# 我的信念

# What I Believe

【英】伯特兰·罗素　著 Bertrand Russell

莫晓敏　译

上海译文出版社

“伯特兰·罗素将宗教归结为一种来自未知的原始恐怖，一种盼着有个亲切的兄长站在我们身旁的欲求。”

——《世纪报》（*The Age*）

“在20世纪所有哲学家中，伯特兰·罗素笔下的英语散文可谓首屈一指。”

——安东尼·霍华德，《泰晤士报》（*The Times*）

# 目　录

# 劳特利奇经典丛书版序

初拾伯特兰·罗素的文字还是五十年前，如今再读，心情颇有几分复杂。二十世纪五十年代中期，在饱受初中学业摧残的少年学子眼里，读罗素的《西方哲学史》（*History of Western Philosophy*）可谓一大乐事。当学校牧师向少年不可知论者使劲儿宣讲阿奎那（Aquinas）的“五例证明神存在”（Five Ways to the knowledge of God’s existence）时，我们正是从《西方哲学史》中拾起武器，予以反击。《为什么我不是基督教徒》（*Why I am not a Christian*）更是反抗权威的珍贵武器。我的舍监认为，罗素的四次婚姻经历败坏了他在性、神与核战争这些议题上发言的可信度，而这愈发确证了我的观点：大多数权威人士都有顽固不化、逻辑不通的毛病，实在不必当一回事。

我并未完全改变我的看法。罗素的四次婚姻，跟他在性、神与核战争这些议题上的发言并不相干；如今我倒是觉得，他的婚姻困境本应令他更留心，才能让追求幸福这件事举重若轻，不过，对于何为美好人生，他所持观念相当耐久。他有不少缺点是他本人作为批评家所不喜的，他的行为也抵触自己信奉的原则：攻敌之至强，而非其至弱。在这些方面，他实不如约翰·密尔可敬。从另一方面来看，他却是更有趣，过去如此，如今依旧。他尤其写得一手好文章，即便是五十元一篇卖给赫斯特报业的豆腐块——为了支持他和第二任妻子创办的比肯山学校（Beacon Hill）——也是才思敏捷，甚至发人深省。要是英国对文学还算上心，就该让青少年好好学习罗素这位散文家中的典范。

第一次世界大战期间，罗素发觉自己具有向听众宣讲的超绝才华。他发自内心地反对战争；作为民主管理联盟[①]的成员，随后又成为反征兵协会[②]的领导人之一，他不懈努力，以求早日结束战争，并劝说美国保持中立，同时保护因宗教或道义原因拒服兵役者：在法庭审理其赦免案时令其不受侵犯，万一最终入狱或入伍则保护其免受虐待。这些行为累他失去了剑桥大

① Union for Democratic Control，1914 年因一战爆发而在英国成立，该团体并非和平主义组织，但是强烈反对征兵、战时管制以及一系列损害公民自由的政策，呼吁公众及政府全面审视战争意图。——译注

② No-Conscription Fellowship，1914 年因一战而成立，创立者入狱后由罗素接任主席。——译注

学三一学院的教职，却也为他打开了新世界的大门。

在那些目标直指早日结束战争以及帮助拒服兵役者免除兵役的无数集会之外，罗素还发表了题为《社会改造原理》（*The Principles of Social Reconstruction*）的一系列讲演，取得惊人成功。如果说罗素有一种单一政治哲学，即可见于该系列讲演集结而成的小书。《我的信念》一书视为理所当然、自不待言的许多内容，在《社会改造原理》中有详尽讨论。其中三大关键前提值得一一分说。

罗素关于人类行为的观点根植于经验主义传统之中。这一传统认为，是欲求（desire）驱使一切行为，而理性（reason）的作用在于告诉我们该如何达成我们的追求，而非我们首先应该追求什么。又或如休谟所言，“理性是并且也应该是情感（passions）的奴隶”[①]，罗素颇为欣赏这份犀利。这并不是在论证通常意义上的“冲动性”（impulsiveness）：罗素认为我们应当用心思考我们的规划，而他希望以更科学的了解，对我们自己的人生规划进行更多反思。这里论证的是，应当试图去理解我们真正的欲求。罗素关于我们欲求之基础的观点并不止于此。他通晓里弗斯（W. H. Rivers）的著作——这位精神病学家曾为西格弗里德·萨松（Siegfried Sassoon）等人治疗弹震神经

① 参见休谟的《人性论》（下册），关文运译，商务印书馆 1980 年版第 453 页。——译注

症，也是在英国采用弗洛伊德之法的第一人。里弗斯觉得弗洛伊德夸大了他的见解，却并不反对我们都远比自己愿意相信的更易受潜在冲动操纵。罗素亦作如是想。

具体而言，罗素大致认为，是人类的本能迫使其走向破坏本身，弗洛伊德关于“求死之心”（death wish）的论述也表明了这一点。在他看来，民族国家之间的战争显然多余无益，故而蠢不可言；他觉得，除了破坏的激情以及参战者为了让他人受难而不惜一切代价、哪怕自身受难的欲求之外，很难相信还能作何解释。然而，相信如此虚无的解释将使罗素的和平主义也随之失效。假如我们下定决心无缘无故地毁掉自己，那么唯一有意义的问题便只剩一个：我们要过多久才能找到将自己尽数消灭的技术。罗素向来不惮出于修辞考虑而大肆描述敌对者屠杀及集体自杀的欲求，不过在他肯做分析的时候，他提出了另一个更为完善的观点。

这一观点就是罗素政治学的第二前提。他在《社会改造原理》中指出，存在两种冲动：占有性冲动要求独占所遭遇的一切事物并引我们相互竞争，而创造性冲动则引我们去寻求在他人不受一丝损害的情况下能够获取的事物。假如德国科学家发现了全新的物理学定理，那么英法科学家能够发现的新定理并不会因此减少；而德国占领西南非洲[①]却大幅削减了英法能够

① 纳米比亚的旧称。——译注

占有的土地，更不要说当地原住民了。假如占有欲与国族荣誉绑在一起，国族荣誉又牵连到对其他国族的凌辱，我们就会招致无穷无尽的战争。要确保和平与幸福，即须鼓励创造性本能，并将占有性本能导向有用的或至少无害的目的。

由此推出第三前提，即罗素意欲宣讲的伦理学。依照最狭义的逻辑，罗素的伦理学毫不倚仗他更广泛的哲学观点。关于这一点，他本人强调了无数次。他指出，严格来讲，任何具体的道德都不可能得到哲学的辩护；哲学所关心的是涉及真理存亡的事件。道德评判是劝诫，是激励，是谴责——是对任一待议行为或性格品质示以好感或敌意的态度表达。“谋杀是恶”并不说明谋杀的性质，而是在斥责谋杀。道德哲学绝不是哲学。这便以生动的形式指出了我们所熟知的一点。罗素常常对道德言说的逻辑进行分析，它们在现代意义上具有明确的哲学意味。不过，不难看出罗素受何驱使。在很长一段时间内他都坚持认为，即便是哲学最抽象的分支——包括逻辑和数学基础——所关心的都是如何将世界本真的样子显现出来。而道德所关心者，与其说是世界的样子，倒不如说是世界应当呈现的样子。

鉴于此，罗素的伦理理论无甚出奇之处。我们的冲动本身并无善恶之分，只不过是些无感情的事实。为善也好，为恶也罢，都取决于这些冲动如何促进或扼制我们自身或他人的其他冲动。我想痛饮一场，这只是一个欲求，却跟我不想宿醉醒来这一欲求有所冲突；也跟你想安全上路的欲求有所冲突，同样受影响的还有我的雇主希望前台接待员神志清醒这一欲求。酩酊大醉之举，说得好听是轻率，多数情况下可谓恶劣。相反，一心帮忙与协作的愿望则不仅能助他人实现目标，且并不阻碍我的其他冲动。于是，我们便将仁慈、助益与好意称为善。对于审慎的、道德容许的行为，我们的标准有赖于我们如何评估罗素所谓的欲求之“共存能力”（compossibility）。我们应当发展那些有助于欲求之满足的欲求，而灭除令其受挫的欲求。

罗素对创造性本能的解释与他对战争的厌恨之间有何关系，几乎不必赘言。同样不必赘言的，还有以欲求之满足来表达他对伦理的解释，似为一种世俗的、自然主义的、享乐主义的伦理理论提供了基础。争议在于，假如罗素前后一致，这就是他本应传递给读者的内容。而实际上并非如此；呈现的结果是世俗的、自然主义的，却非（大体上）对享乐主义的辩护。罗素颇肖其教父约翰·密尔，他所拥护的高尚理想并不那么注重追求日常意义上的幸福——譬如说勇气，对真理的热爱以及对于其间自然世界的一种无涉功用的关注。且不论对错，罗素同意密尔的看法，即不满足的苏格拉底也比心满意足的愚人更好。《我的信念》一书为之辩护的是对于真理的无私追求，此乃美好人生的一大要素，而罗素对宗教最激烈的控诉莫过于：宗教是对宇宙之荒凉的怯懦回应。

《我的信念》跻身于一系列篇幅极短的小书（按出版社的

说法是小册子）之中，书系名为“今日与明日”。小书虽小，着眼却大：女性的未来，战争，人口，科学，机器，道德，戏剧，诗歌，艺术，音乐，性……多拉·罗素（Dora Russell）写了《希帕蒂娅》（*Hypatia*）为女性解放辩护，而罗素写了书系中的两本小册子，《我的信念》正是其二。对于未来科学能给人类带来什么，霍尔丹（J. B. S. Haldane）在《代达罗斯》（*Daedalus*）中提出了乐观的看法；罗素则通过《伊卡洛斯》（*Icarus*）予以犀利回应。他指出，代达罗斯之子伊卡洛斯学会了如何飞行，却不能明智应用。[①] 既然科学作为对世界进行理性探索的果实，只能告诉我们如何达成我们的目标，那么科学进步最惊人的成果极有可能就是将战争变为全球大屠杀。倘能免于此难，我们要么将随着大规模官僚机构接管世界而无聊至死，要么任自己转化为赫胥黎的《美丽新世界》——此书的灵感来源大概也是《伊卡洛斯》——所描绘的良民，通过基因改造来适应我们的社会角色，并灌药实现一切优生学无法达成的效果。

由于罗素是反核武器运动的发起人之一，又颇热衷于大书

① 古希腊传说中，迷宫建造者代达罗斯被米诺斯王囚禁在克里特岛，遂用鸟羽蜂蜡制成翅膀，与子出逃。伊卡洛斯一时忘形飞高，激怒了太阳神，以致蜡融羽落而坠海。两书主标题分别借用了以上传说象征，副标题均为“科学的未来”：霍尔丹描绘了未来科学发现用于促进人类福祉的诱人图景，罗素则担心人类对科学的滥用将导致毁灭性灾难。——译注

特书核战争的可怖之处，我们很容易忘记他对于人类未来的恐惧一开始并非来自核武器，而是一战的工业化战争以及随后二十世纪三十年代远程轰炸机的出现。《伊卡洛斯》自恃机智而近尖刻，极为不公地将绝大多数掌权者归类为邪恶鲁莽的存在，对于人类前景则满怀悲观。这并非罗素最后一次表露此观点：作为世间乱象的罪魁祸首，人类自我消灭或许倒是好事一桩。

《我的信念》意在矫正平衡，这一点昭然若揭。其行文如此清醒而风趣，对将要亲自享用阅读罗素之乐趣的读者解释其内容，未免显得可笑。想要有所助益，倒不如将罗素关于宗教话题的独特立场略述几句，或者讲讲《我的信念》一书如何以明确的乐观结论提出了科学的创造性可能而非毁灭性可能，从而逆转了《伊卡洛斯》投下的阴影。

世界上有两种无神论者——罗素称自己为“不可知论者”，这暗示着神并非不可能以某种形式存在，然而他非常确定神本身并不存在，视他为无神论者似乎更妥帖。第一种无神论者的观点有时可以表述为“神并不存在，我恨他”；他们希望神存在，以便向其倾诉抱怨宇宙之荒谬。伦纳德·伍尔夫（Leonard Woolf）有一次说，他想向神质问人类消化系统的构造，这项管道工程看上去异常笨拙。第二种无神论者与其说是愤怒，不如说是无聊；他们无法理解，为神与灵或你口中的任意超自然体编出种种故事来能有什么用途；这些故事完全不能增进我们对世界的理解，还会引发思维混乱，并为相互迫害提供土壤，我们人类当中的不和与暴力又何需更多刺激呢。为此两种皆有可能，但两种同时都是，就颇为尴尬了。

罗素充当第一种无神论者的频率和充当第二种的频率相差无几，不过《我的信念》大体上从第二种角度出发写就。无论如何，恰是第一种无神论提供了大部分情感力量，即使在这篇文章里也是如此。那些无法理解为什么会有人费心编造故事讲述宇宙起源及人类行止的无神论者，或许本应对此话题保持缄默并投身于其他事务。罗素却几乎总是抓住一切机会对虔信者恶语相向——他也收到了同等回敬。①

这并不难解释：人类存在就是惨事一桩——就算罗素对此还不够坚定，至少也是半信半疑了；生活本该是美好的，可大多时候并非如此。因此，我们完全不敢想象，会有某个存在故意创造出这样的一个世界，我们在其中始终如一地承受焦虑，不是死于暴力，就是死于疾病折磨，心碎与失望带来的剧烈苦痛远远超出了因爱与心愿得偿而生的喜悦。若世间有神，那么他或她或它或他们应已厌腻了反人性之罪。虔信者犯下崇拜邪恶之罪，要么是因为过于怯懦而不敢直面神正是罪人这一事实，要么是扭曲的道德感令他们真心相信强权即公理。

《我的信念》所持的无神论属于不那么激烈的第二种。这

① 此处有一双关：speak unkindly/repaid in kind。——译注

世界所为人知的一切，就是科学所揭露的内容；猜想我们会永存不朽，或者在宇宙这架装置的背后还站着某个幽灵般的钟表匠，均无依据。尽管如此，针对宗教在伦理与政治当中所扮演的角色仍有一些尖锐的指责。罗素还特别借此机会控诉，宗教人士竟支持通过战争和饥荒来节育，却千方百计阻止当时玛格丽特·桑格（Margaret Sanger）等人提倡的避孕节育法。当然，罗素以通过此类争执激怒虔信者为乐。他的许多读者谴责他频频显露的不公，然而，在他的修辞策略背后实有其严肃意义。

那就是，许多宗教——尤其是基督教——对于性行为有一种强迫性关注。在罗素看来，基督教徒不去操心如何让人们过上还算幸福的生活，并养育够多（却勿过多）健康快乐、教养良好的孩子，反倒一心阻挠而非帮助人们静心思考这些问题。将近八十年过去，如今再回过头去看当年美国的反堕胎人士，就很容易与罗素产生共鸣了。敬神者后来向罗素报了仇，那是一九四〇年，纽约法庭以他教授“不道德”为由，撤销了他在纽约市立学院的职位。他的敌人所举证据当中，就有《我的信念》一书。

对基于宗教虔信的道德，在罗素给出的反对理由当中至少有一项不仅仅适用于那些狭义上以宗教为依据的道德。罗素仇视一切以规则为依据的伦理形式。他认为，道德在人生中作用甚微，这倒是没错。譬如说，照顾孩子的时候，没有人会去翻找父母监护职责的规则；他们是受爱驱使——又或不是——不管哪样，道德在其中全无作用。假如他们缺乏恰当的情感，道德教化也无法改造他们；而假如他们有所触动，道德立场就是多余的。罗素尤其敌视这样的思想：道德由规则组成，这些规则的设定者则是某个权威——无论是神或是超我。规则是僵死的，而罗素非常确定，关于我们行动的理性思想必须具备足可应对万事变迁的灵活性。

最后，该谈谈科学在这一切当中扮演的角色了。在《我的信念》一书里，罗素坚定地表示，我们不应“遵从”（respect）自然，而应研究自然如何运作，以令自然之力为人类所用。对此应当提出两点。第一，如我们所见，对人类会否将科学用于正当目的而非邪恶目的，罗素是举棋不定的；《伊卡洛斯》多考虑我们滥用科学的可能性，《我的信念》则多勉励我们正当运用科学。第二，罗素在很大程度上依赖于以下对比：宗教与道德指的是缺乏任何理性根基或以残忍为代价满足人类口味的僵死规则，而科学则是对于事物因果的点滴理解。他所愿鼓励促进的，正是科学的态度。

他并非一直这样迫切叮嘱读者切勿遵从自然。四十年后，他不无苦涩地批评人类用可能向敌人发射核弹头的轨道卫星玷污天宇的迫切渴望，并指责美国实用主义者约翰·杜威（John Dewey）声称自然充斥着人类目的这一言论实乃“亵渎”。这并不是一个简单的矛盾。罗素从不认为自然提供了道德标准，或自然本身就是我们行为规范的来源；当他在《我的信念》一书里谴责“遵从”时，那正是他的用意所在。与此同时，他总觉得宇宙的无边空虚是如此动人——令人惊悸，也给人安慰。这一情感令许多读者判定，罗素终究是一名极度虔信的思想者。设令如此，罗素便是那众多虔信思想者中的一员，这些人感到一切实际宗教都无法容纳他们意欲表达的情绪。

阿兰·瑞安

二〇〇三年

# 引　言

在这本小书里，我将试述我如何理解人在宇宙间的地位，在追求美好人生这一方面又有着怎样的可能性。在《伊卡洛斯》当中，我阐明了我的恐惧；在接下来的篇章里，则吐露了希望。其间矛盾，无非表象。在天文学领域之外，人类还不曾掌握预测未来的本领；在人间世事之中，我们不难看到那些带来幸福的力量，同样也有带来苦痛的力量。我们无从知晓何者将会取胜，但要明智行事，任何一方都不可忽视。

伯·罗

一九二五年一月一日

# 第一篇　自然与人

人，乃是自然的一员，而非自然的对立者。人的思想及其形体举止，莫不依从那同样定义着星辰与原子运动的种种定律。较之于人，物质世界是如此庞大——超过了但丁时代的设想，却又似不及一百年前人们眼中那样大。无论是从前还是往后，整体还是局部，科学似乎都到了极限。人们认为，宇宙是空间上的有限域，而光能够在几亿年间穿梭往返。人们认为，物质由电子和质子组成，它们体积有限，在世间的数量也相当有限。其变化或许并不像过去人们以为的那样连续不断，而是由急动度[①]推进，这一急动度有一个跌不穿的最低值。这些变

① 急动度（jerk），又称变加速度、加加速度或冲动度，是描述加速度变化快慢的广义力学物理量。粗略而言，由急动度引起的运动是无序的，即混沌。——译注

化的定律显然可以归纳为区区几条通用原则，当人们知晓这个世界的点滴历史，这些原则便可定其过去与未来。

自然科学正是如此走向完满，同时也将由此丧失趣味。一旦获知约束着电子与质子运动的种种定律，余下不过是地理学，是一系列特定事实——其于世界历史某一段当中的分布已经给出。足以决定世界历史的事实总量或许是有限的；理论上讲，可将其全部记录下来，写入一部巨书，藏在萨默塞特府①，旁边连接一台计算器，只消摇动手柄，就能让发问者得知在这些记录时间之外发生的事实。很难想象世界上还有什么比这更无趣，或是更有悖于未完成的发现所给予的热烈喜悦。那就像是攀上高山之巅却一无所获，只找到一间售卖姜啤的餐厅，深陷雾中却备有无线电装置。在阿梅斯②的时代，乘法表或许也曾激动人心。

至于这个本身无趣的物质世界，人正是其中一员。他的身体亦如其他物质一般由电子与质子组成，在我们的知识范畴内，它们与那些并不构成动植物的基本粒子一样，遵循相同的法则。有人坚持说，生理学永远不能归结为物理学，不过他们

① 萨默塞特府（Somerset House），泰晤士河畔大型建筑，一度容纳伦敦大学国王学院、皇家学会、文物学会、皇家艺术研究院等文教组织，至今仍是伦敦重要的艺术中心。——译注

② 阿梅斯（Ahmes），古埃及书吏，他抄录的《莱因德纸草书》是世界上最古老的数学著作之一，约成于公元前 1650 年。——译注

的论证不太有说服力，就此判断他们错了似乎也不算莽撞。我们所谓的“思想”似乎依赖于大脑中的沟回组织，正如旅行依赖于道路和铁路。用于思考的能量似有其化学根源；譬如说，缺碘会让一个聪明人变成傻子。心理现象似与物质结构紧密相关。若真如此，我们很难想象单独一个电子或质子会“思考”；还不如指望一个人独自去踢一场球赛呢。我们也无法想象个人的思考在肉体死亡之后还能继续，因为死亡毁坏了脑组织，并消散了作用于脑沟回的能量。

神与永存不朽作为基督教的核心教义，在科学上却得不到支持。它们哪一个都称不上宗教之根本，因为均不见于佛教。（谈及永存不朽，这一论断在无限制的表述中或许会有所误导，但归根结底是正确的。）但我们西方人多视其为神学中不可再简化的底限。毋庸置疑，人们将继续抱有此类信念，因为它们确实令人愉快，恰如视自身为善而视仇敌为恶一样令人愉快。但就我自身而言，以上立场概无根基。我不会假装自己有本事证明世间无神。同样，我也无法证明撒旦乃是虚构。基督教的神或许存在；奥林匹斯山、古埃及或巴比伦诸神或许亦然。然而，在这许多假说当中，并没有哪一个比另一个更具有可能性：它们都位于可能性的知识范畴之外，因此也没有理由去考虑其中任何一个。这一问题将不再展开，因为我在别处已有探讨。[①]

① 参见拙作《莱布尼茨的哲学》（*Philosophy of Leibniz*，1900），第十五章。

至于个人之永存不朽这一问题，立足点则稍有不同。在此，两方面的证据都有可能。人属于科学所关注的日常世界，而决定其存在的条件是可察的。一滴水不能永存不朽；它会分解为氧和氢。因此，假如一滴水坚持自己具备的水的特性，哪怕经过分解也不会消散，那么我们多半就要心生疑虑了。同样的道理，我们知道大脑也不能永存不朽，生命体积蓄的能量将会于死亡时消散，由此无法再支撑集体行动。一切证据都表明，我们所知道的精神生命离不开大脑的构造以及机体能量的积蓄。因此，设想精神生命将随着机体生命的消亡而逝去，也是合情合理的。这一论证固然只是一种可能性，却和大多数科学结论所依据的根基一样坚实。

要驳斥这一结论，可以从好几个不同角度出发。心灵研究（psychical research）声称，关于死后意识不灭（survival），他们有切实的科学证据，且其过程无疑基本具备科学正确性。此类证据可能极为强有力，使得任何具备科学态度的人都无从拒绝。不过，证据的分量当然取决于死后意识不灭这一假说的先行可能性。对于任何现象的解释总会有不同的方式，我们自当从中选择先行不可能性最低的一种。那些认为我们死后意识可能不灭的人，也将乐于视之为心灵现象的最佳阐释。反过来，那些视之为无理的人，则将另觅他说。迄今为止，心灵研究所引证的那些支持死后意识不灭的证据，在我看来，尚不及与其对立的生理证据有力。但我完全同意它随时有可能变得更为有力，设令如此，不相信死后意识不灭就是一种非科学态度了。

然而，与永存不朽不同，肉体死亡而意识不灭可能只意味着心灵死亡的延迟。而人类之所欲信仰者，乃是永存不朽。永存不朽的信徒将会反对（如我所用的）生理论证，理由是灵魂与肉体完全分离，而灵魂并不等同于它通过我们的肉体器官表现出来的经验主义形态。我相信这是一种形而上的迷信。心与物同，皆是为特定目的而设的适用术语，而非终极现实。电子与质子就像灵魂一样，均为逻辑虚构（logical fiction）；实则各为一段历史、一系列事件，而非单一连续的实体。至于灵魂，生长这一事实可令其显露无疑。不论是谁，只要想一想受孕期、妊娠期和婴儿期，就不可能真正相信在此过程中灵魂是什么不可分割的、完美又完备的存在。显而易见，就像肉体一样，灵魂也会生长，它既源自精子也源自卵子，因此不可能是不可分割的。这并非唯物主义：只不过是承认一切有意义的东西都是一种组织，而非原始物质。

形而上学家曾提出大量论证，意欲证明灵魂定然永存不朽。有一项简单的测试足以推翻所有这些论证——它们都同样证明灵魂定然遍及一切空间。但由于我们对肥胖的欲求并不像对长寿那样迫切，这些形而上学家没有一个注意到他们的推理在此方面的应用。这一事例体现了欲求的神奇力量如何蒙上了聪明人的眼睛，将他们引向本应昭然若揭的谬论。我相信，假若我们不惧死亡，永存不朽的观念甚至都不会产生。

恐惧是宗教教义的根基，对于人类生活的方方面面而言也是如此。人类的恐惧，无论是个体性的还是群体性的，支配了我们大部分社会生活，但却是对自然的恐惧令宗教得以产生。如我们所见，心物二元对立或多或少是一种虚幻；不过，有一种更重要的对立，那就是我们的欲求能够影响的事物与不能影响的事物。两者之间的界限并不分明，亦非一成不变——随着科学发展，越来越多的事物得以纳入人类控制范围。即便如此，有些事物无疑位于此范围之外，其中包括一切关于我们世界的宏大事实，那些涉及天文学的事实。在某种程度上，可供我们塑造以满足我们欲求的，只有那些在我们地表或其附近发生的事实。即便是在地表，我们的力量也相当有限。最重要的是，我们无法阻止死亡，即便我们往往可以延缓其到来。

宗教就是一种意在克服对立的尝试。假如说世界由神操控，而祈祷又能感动神，那么全能之中就有了属于我们的一份。过去，神迹应祈祷而生；天主教教会至今如是，但新教已失去这一能力。然而，神迹不再，倒也无妨，因为天意已定：自然法则的运作将产生最佳结果。故此，对神的信仰仍是要将自然世界人性化，并使人们感到自然力量实乃同盟。同样，永存不朽也消除了死亡的恐怖。那些相信他们死后将永享极乐的人应能直面死亡而无畏，不过，医务人员应当庆幸，这不一定总是会发生。然而，这确实多多少少安抚了人类的恐惧，虽则未必能带来彻底的缓解。

宗教，盖因有其根植于恐怖的源头，遂将某些特定的恐惧奉为高贵，又令人们以为这类恐惧并不可耻。由此，它给人类带来了极大损害：一切恐惧皆是恶。我相信我死后会腐朽，我的自我不留一丝一毫在人间。我并不年轻，我热爱生活。但对于一想到灵肉湮灭就惊悸不已这种行为，我却要嗤之以鼻。哪怕注定完结，幸福仍是真实的幸福；就算不能久长，思想与爱也不会失却价值。多少人在绞刑架前表现高傲；同样的高傲想必也能教我们诚心思考人在这世间的身份。在习惯了传统的人性化神话所造就的一室温暖惬意之后，大敞的科学之窗固然会让我们打个冷战，但新鲜的空气终将带来生机，广阔的空间也自有其壮美。

自然哲学是一回事，价值哲学又是另一回事。两者混为一谈，百害而无一利。我们认为好的，我们所应喜好的，都与事物本真的样子没有任何关系，而后者是自然哲学的问题。另一方面，不能因为非人类世界不赋予某些事物价值就不允许我们赋予那些事物价值，也不能因为某些事物是“自然法则”就迫使我们心悦诚服。我们无疑是自然的一员，依据自然科学家才刚刚开始探索的法则，自然一手造就我们的欲求，造就我们的希望与恐惧。在此意义上，我们是自然的一员，我们服从自然，我们是自然法则的结果，也是其最终的牺牲品。

自然哲学切不可过度世俗化；于其而言，地球不过是漫漫银河亿万小小星体之中的一颗小小行星。为了得出让这颗微不足道的行星上存在的小小寄生物高兴的结果，而去歪曲自然哲学，该是多么荒唐可笑。作为哲学的生机论（Vitalism）以及演化论，在这方面暴露出分寸感与逻辑相干性的不足。那些仅就我们个体而言值得关注的生命事实，它们却为之赋予宇宙层面的意义，而非局限于地球表面的意义。作为宇宙哲学的乐观主义与悲观主义，同样表现出朴素的人本主义；就我们在自然哲学之中所知，广大世界既无谓好与坏，也无意给我们喜或悲。所有这类哲学都源于妄自尊大，最好的改正办法莫过于多学一点天文学。

价值哲学的情况却截然相反。自然不过是我们想象事物之中的一部分；真实也好，想象也罢，一切皆可任由我们评估，并无任何外在标准能断言我们的评价有误。我们自己就是终极的、不可辩驳的价值仲裁者，而在价值的世界里，自然不过是某一部分。故此，在这个世界里，我们比自然更伟大。在价值的世界里，自然本身是中立的，无谓好坏，无须褒贬。是我们创造了价值，我们的欲求则赋予价值。在这个领域之中，我们就是王，如果我们向自然低头，我们的王权就会有所贬损。美好人生应当由我们来判定，而非自然——就连人格化为神的自然也不行。

## 第二篇　美好人生

纵观不同年代，遍览不同人群，对于美好人生的设想多姿多态，各式各样。在某种程度上，这些分歧可以通过论证来检验；这时候，分歧出现在人们达成给定目的的手段上。有人认为，监禁是扼制罪行的良方；也有人觉得教育更佳。一旦有了足够证据，这一类分歧是可以解决的。但某些分歧却不能这样检验。托尔斯泰谴责一切战争；也有人觉得，士兵若是为正义而战，其一生便可称高尚。就目的而论，这里或许涉及真正的分歧。那些歌颂士兵的人通常将惩罚罪人本身视为善事；托尔斯泰则不然。就此而言，一切论证均无效用。故此，我无法证明我关于美好人生的观点是正确的；我只能阐明我的观点，并希望与我共鸣者多多益善。我的观点如下：

美好人生是启之以爱、导之以知的人生。

知与爱两者均无止境；故此，无论人生有多美好，我们总是可以想象出更好的人生。有爱而无知，或有知而无爱，都不可造就美好人生。中世纪时，乡间瘟疫横行，教士劝民众聚在教堂，祈祷救赎降临；结果传染病情在祈愿者的拥挤人群中迅速蔓延。这便是有爱而无知的案例。最近发生的战争则是有知而无爱的案例。两个案例的结局都是大规模死亡。

虽则爱与知两者皆不可少，在某种意义上，爱却是更为根本的那一个，因为爱会引领聪明的人为造福所爱之人而求知。但如果人们不够聪明，他们就会对道听途说心满意足、深信不疑，那么天大的好心也能办成坏事。医药或许可以为此提供最佳案例。对于病人来说，一个能干的医生比最忠诚的朋友更有用，而对于社区卫生来说，医疗知识的进展比耳目闭塞的慈善事业更有助益。虽然如此，仁慈之心仍不可少，否则也许只有富人能受益于科学发现。

爱之一字，包含多种感受（feelings）；选而用之，乃是我刻意所为，因为我希望将这些感受兼收并蓄。爱作为一种情感（emotion）——这正是我所说的爱，因为“基于原则”的爱在我看来并不真实——在两极之间摇摆：一极是观照中的纯粹快感（delight），另一极则是纯粹的仁慈（benevolence）。涉及无生命体时，只有快感降临；对一处风景或一支奏鸣曲，我们无法生出仁慈之心。这种享乐想必正是艺术之源。比起惯用功利主义眼光看待事物的成人，它在年幼的孩童身上通常更为强烈。它在我们对人类的感受当中大有作为，当我们将人类仅仅视为审美观照的客体时，有些人具备取悦的魅力，有些人则不然。

爱的另一极是纯粹的仁慈。人们为了帮助麻风病人而牺牲性命；在这种情况下，他们怀有的爱不可能具备任何审美快感。父母之爱通常伴随着因孩子的外貌而产生的喜悦，但是当这一要素彻底不存在时，父母之爱依旧强烈。将母亲对生病孩子的关怀称为“仁慈”，似乎有些古怪，因为我们惯以该词描述一种带有九分哄骗意味的苍白情感。但是，很难找到另一个词来形容这种对他人福利的欲求。事实上，就父母之情而言，这一欲求足以达到任何强度。就其他情况而言，强度则远远不及；甚至可以这么看，一切利他的情感很有可能都是父母之情的一种漫溢，有时又是一种升华。苦于找不到更好的词，我且将这种情感称为“仁慈”。但我想要明确一点，这里所说的是一种情感而非原则，我也无意带入常常与该词挂钩的任何优越感。“同情”一词或许能够覆盖我的一部分所指，但又缺乏我想要引入的行动要素。

最完满的爱是快感与善愿这两大要素不可分割的合体。父母因孩子有貌亦有成而生的喜悦，即是两大要素并存；最好的性爱也是如此。但在性爱之中，仁慈只能依托稳定的占有关系而存在，否则嫉妒就会摧而毁之，同时或许还能平添几分观照的快感。有快感而无善愿，可能失之严酷；有善愿而无快感，则极易表现为冷淡与轻微的优越。希望被爱的人，总是希望自己收获两者兼得的爱，极端弱势的情况除外，例如婴儿和危重疾病。在这些情况下，仁慈或许就是人们所欲求的一切。反之，在极端强势的情况下，比起仁慈，人们所欲求的更多是钦慕：这就是那些君王与知名美人的心态。我们对于他人善愿的欲求，取决于我们感觉自身需要帮助或他人对我们造成威胁的程度。这至少可以算是这种情形下的生物逻辑，但对于人生却不尽然。我们欲求感情，是为了逃离孤独感，为了获得所谓的“理解”。这是一种同情，而不仅仅是仁慈；那些在感情上满足我们的人，绝不能只是对我们怀有善愿，而必须知晓我们的幸福之所在。不过这属于美好人生的另一要素：知。

在完美世界之中，有情众生互为最完满之爱的客体，这种完满由快感、仁慈和理解密不可分地融为一体。这并不意味着，在此现实世界之中，对所遭遇的一切有情众生，我们都应当试着付出这样的感受。其中会有许多客体让我们无法产生快感，因为他们令人厌恶；假如我们为了勉强在他们身上看出美而扭曲自己的天性，那只会损害我们本身对于天性以为美的事物的敏感度。且不谈人类，世上还有跳蚤、臭虫和虱子。要在对这些生物的观照中获得快感，我们恐怕得像古舟子[①]那样先受尽磨难才行。诚然，某些圣人也会称之为“神之珠”，但这些人的快感来自展示他们自身神圣的机会。

仁慈较易广为延扩，可纵是仁慈也有其限度。假设有个男人想要娶一位女子，当他发现另外有个人也想娶她，这时我们不会说他放弃更好：我们应当视之为公平竞争的场合。然而，他对情敌的感受不可能是彻头彻尾的仁慈。我想，在各式各样的美好人生之中，我们必须首先将动物活力和动物本能设定为某种基础；舍此，人生就会变得乏味无趣。文明应是在此基础上做出的补充，而非取代；苦行的圣人和超然的哲人恰因疏忽于此，而未能成为完整的人。这样的人，少少几个，或可丰富群落；但若人人如此，世界将无聊至死。

出于这些考量，快感这一要素作为最好的爱的一部分，颇受注重。在此现实世界中，快感难免有所选择，令我们无法对全体人类产生同样的感受。一般说来，当快感和仁慈有所冲突时，必须通过妥协让步来达成和解，而非任何一方的彻底臣服。本能也有其权利，假如我们刻意扭曲本能，一旦超过一定限度，就会遭遇微妙的反弹。故此，要追求美好人生，须将人类可能性的极限铭记在心。不过如此一来，我们就再次回到了

① 典出柯尔律治长诗《古舟子咏》。一名老水手在行船中恩将仇报，射杀了引路的信天翁，神明震怒，降下天罚。老水手历尽生死劫难之际，看到海蛇，顿悟生命之美，并为之祈福，终获宽恕。——译注

知的必要性这个问题。

谈及作为人生组成之一的知，我所想到的并不是伦理知识，而是科学知识和关于特定事实的知识。严格说来，我不觉得伦理知识这种东西真的存在。假如我们欲求达成某个目的，知识或可为我们指路，这种知识大概可以勉强充作伦理知识。但我并不认为我们能够决定某种行为的对错，除非参考到最终可能产生的影响。一个有待达成的目的应该如何设法达成，这是科学要解决的问题。一切道德规则都必须经受检验：考察它们是否有助于实现我们所欲求的目的。在此，我说的是“我们所欲求的目的”，而非“我们应欲求的目的”。我们“应”欲求的目的，不过是他人希望我们欲求的目的。通常是权威——父母、教师、警察和法官——希望我们有此欲求。如果你跟我说“你应如此如此”，这番言辞的原动力在于我欲求你的认可——或许还要加上与你的认可与否相关联的赏或罚。既然一切行为皆源自欲求，那么伦理观念显然无关紧要，唯有对欲求产生影响时除外。而伦理观念产生影响，正是通过对认可的欲求以及对不认可的恐惧。这些都是强大的社会力量，假如我们希望实现任何社会目标，自当竭力将这些力量争取过来。当我说行为道德应根据可能引发的后果来评判时，我想看到的是对可能实现我们所欲求之社会目标的行为予以认可，对相反的行为则不予认可。当前，这一点还无法实现；某些决定认可与否的传统规则并不顾及后果。不过，这是我们下一篇要讨论的话题。

在简单情况下，理论伦理的冗余性是有目共睹的。比方说，设想一下，你的孩子病了。爱驱使你产生治病的欲求，而科学告诉你如何达成。其间并不存在一个让伦理理论证明你的孩子应当治好的中间阶段。你的行动直接来自欲求，指向一个目的，以及关于手段的知识。这也同样适用于一切行动，无论好坏。目的各自有别，知识也是在某些情况下相较而言更为适用。但是，我们想不到什么办法让人们去做他们不想做的事情，只能用赏罚体制来改变他们的欲求，而社会认可与否并不是其中最无说服力的一种。故此，法制道德家所面临的问题在于：赏罚体制该如何安排，才能保证立法机关所欲求的最大化效果？如果我说立法机关怀有恶欲，不过是指其欲求与我所归属的那部分社会的欲求有所冲突。在人类欲求之外，并无道德标准。

故此，令伦理区别于科学的并非任何特殊知识，而不过是欲求。伦理中所需知识与他处所需者并无不同；特别之处在于，人们欲求达到某些特定目的，而正确行为就是有助于此的行为。当然，如果正确行为的定义要获得普遍支持，其目的必须符合人类之大多数的欲求。假如我将正确行为定义为增加我的个人收入，读者就会表示反对。任何伦理论证的全部有效性都来自其科学部分，那就是证明某种行为——而非其他行为——作为一种手段，能够达到人们普遍欲求的目的。不过，我要将伦理论证和伦理教育区分开来。后者涉及特定欲求的强化与其他欲求的弱化。这一过程是截然不同的，稍后我们将另行讨论。

现在，对于本篇开头提出的主旨，即美好人生的定义，我们可以给出更准确的解释了。当我说美好人生由爱构成，而爱由知来导引时，激励我的欲求是：我欲尽我所能去过这样的生活，并见证他人也照此生活；这一声明的逻辑含义在于，在人类照此生活的社会里，相较于爱更少或知更少的社会，将有更多欲求得到满足。我并不是说此种人生即“美德”，也不是说其反面即“罪恶”，因为在我看来，这些都是缺乏科学辩护的概念。

## 第三篇　道德准则

道德的实际需要产生于欲求之间的冲突，可以是不同的人的欲求，也可以是同一个人不同时期的欲求，甚至是同一个人同一时期的欲求。某人欲饮酒，又欲胜任明早的工作。假如他采用的做法不能使其欲求获得更大的总体满足，我们就会视之为不道德。我们对过分放纵或不计后果的人评价不佳，即使他们伤害的只有自己。边沁认为，道德整体可能起源于“觉醒的利己主义”，并且，一个人的行动如果总是着眼于自身的最大满足，那么从长远来看，他的行动将会永远是正确的。我无法认同这一观点。世间亦有通过观赏酷刑而获得强烈喜悦的暴君；假如审慎令其着眼于他日更进一步的受难，从而饶过牺牲品的性命，我也无法为之称颂。虽则如此，在其他条件不变的前提下，审慎是美好人生的组成之一。就连鲁宾逊也免不了需要辛勤劳作、自我控制和远见卓识的时候，这些都得算是道德品质，因为它们增强了他的总体满足，与此同时，又不以损害他人为代价。对于幼童培养，这一部分道德作用极大，因为幼童几无考虑未来的倾向。倘若嗣后在他们的人生中，这一部分道德得以践行，人间将很快变作天堂，因为这就足以遏止战争这种激情之举而非理性之举。虽则如此，尽管审慎极为重要，它还算不上道德最令人关注的部分，也不是能引发知性问题的部分，因其所诉求的一切均不超出自我利益之外。

审慎所未容纳的那一部分道德，本质上可类比于法律或团体规则。这是令人们面对其欲求有所冲突的可能性，而在同一社区中共同生活的方法。然而，在此可能出现两种截然不同的方法。一为刑法之法，即通过某种方式将挫败他人欲求的行为指向令人不喜的后果，从而达到表面和谐，仅此而已。此亦为社会谴责之法：受到自己所在社会轻视也是一种惩罚形式，为免于此，许多人都不愿让人知道自己侵犯了他们集体的章程。不过，还有一种更根本的方法，一旦成功，即可带来远远更为令人满意的结果。那就是改造人的特性与欲求，尽最大可能，使此人欲求之达成与他人欲求之达成相合，从而将冲突的机会降到最低限度。爱之所以比恨更好，就是因为爱为所涉之人的欲求带来和谐，而非冲突。两人之间有爱，则成败与共；而两人若彼此憎恨，则你死我活。

美好人生应启以爱，导以知——假如我们这话说得不错，那么显然任何群体的道德章程都不会是终极的、自足的，而必检之验之，察其所行是否一如智慧与仁慈所指。道德章程并非一向完美无缺。阿兹特克人因忧心太阳将黯而食人肉，他们视此为痛苦的责任。[①] 这是他们的科学出了错；假如他们对献祭的牺牲者有那么一丝一毫的爱，或许本应察觉这一科学上的错误。某些部落会将十岁到十七岁之间的少女幽闭于暗处，因为害怕太阳之光令其受孕。然而，我们现代的道德章程肯定不包含任何与此相类的未开化习俗吧？我们肯定只会制止那些真正有害的事物，至少是那些极度令人作呕、没有一个正派人能为之辩护的事物吧？我却不敢作此断言。

当今道德乃是功利主义与迷信行为的古怪混合，然而迷信部分更为强势，这是很自然的，因为迷信正是道德准则之源。起初，某些举止被视为神明所不喜，并为法律所禁止，因为神明之怒往往加诸群体，而非仅仅降在有罪的个体头上。是以有了“罪”（sin）的观念，即为神明之不喜者。至于某些举止何以令神明不喜，却没有给出相应的理由；例如，很难说明，为何“用山羊羔母的奶煮山羊羔”会令神明不喜。但根据《启示

① 根据阿兹特克传说，须以活人血肉供奉神明，方能维持太阳每日东升的能量，保证世界正常运转。——译注

录》，事实就是如此。[①] 有时候，对神谕的解读很是古怪。例如，我们收到指示说礼拜六不可劳作，而新教徒将此理解为礼拜天不可游乐。然而，新的禁令获得了和旧的禁令一样至高无上的权威。

一个持有科学人生观的人显然不会被《圣经》经文或教会教义吓倒。他不会满足于宣称“如此这般的行为是有罪的，讨论结束”。他会叩问这一行为是否有害，抑或正相反，有害的恰是认定这一行为有害的信念。于是他会发现，尤其是在关于性这一方面，我们当今的道德极大部分源自纯粹的迷信。他也会发现，这一迷信与阿兹特克人的迷信一般无异，都包涵着无谓的残忍，并且，当人们为他们对旁人的善意感受所驱动时，这一迷信将会一扫而空。然而，传统道德的卫道士往往不是心怀善意的人，从教会显贵的尚武好战态度之中或可窥而知之。我们不禁揣度，他们之所以重视道德，只是为了给自己强加苦痛的欲求找到一个合法出口；罪人即狩猎对象，因此不须宽容！

让我们来追溯一段从胚胎到坟墓的平凡人生，并留意迷信的道德如何在其中强加了本应可免之难。我要从胚胎开始，是

① 当时的异教仪式常用羊奶煮羊羔献祭神明，以求土地肥沃。“不可用山羊羔母的奶煮山羊羔”这一诫谕在《圣经·旧约》中重复了三次（分别见于《出埃及记》23：19及34：26；《申命记》14：21）。在《启示录》中，耶稣基督就是神的羔羊，背负世人的罪孽。——译注

因为迷信的影响在这一阶段尤为显著。假如父母未婚，孩子就会蒙受污名——显然万万不应至此。假如父母一方患有性病，孩子很可能会遗传下来。假如父母已经养了太多孩子，家庭入不敷出，那么与之俱来的就是贫困、少食、拥挤，甚至很可能出现乱伦。然而，大多数道德家仍然认为，最好还是不要让为人父母者学会通过避孕来避免这一苦难。[①] 为了取悦这些道德家，万万千千本不应来此世间的人陷入饱受折磨的一生，只因不以繁育后代为欲求的性行为被视作邪恶，而一旦有此欲求便不再邪恶，即便由此而来的后代在人力所及的范围内必定受苦。骤然受死，随后成为食物，这就是阿兹特克人献祭牺牲者的命运，而论其程度，远远不及一个生于惨境、身染性病的孩子身受之苦。然而，大主教和政治家们以道德之名蓄意强加的苦难还要更为壮大。他们哪怕仍有一丝一毫对孩子的爱或怜悯，必不能坚持这极度残忍的道德章程。

在初生以及婴儿期，普通孩子所受之苦多出自经济之困，迷信之害尚且不及。当家境宽裕的女性养育孩子时，她们拥有最好的医生、最好的护理、最好的饮食、最好的休息和最好的

① 幸运的是，这一切已成为过去。如今，绝大多数新教与犹太教领袖都不再反对节制生育。罗素的陈述极为精确地描绘了 1925 年的事态。尤为意味深长的是，除去少数例外，所有支持避孕的伟大先驱——Francis Place，Richard Carlile，Charles Knowlton，Charles Bradlaugh 以及玛格丽特·桑格——无一不是杰出的自由思想者。——原编注

锻炼。工薪阶层女性则无法享此福利，她们的孩子也常因此而夭折。在关怀母亲这方面，当局也曾办下些许小事，但只是勉强而为。当局为节省开支而削减了对哺乳期母亲的供奶，与此同时，却肯投入大笔经费为交通稀少的富人住宅区修路。他们必知，下此决定，等若宣判诸多工薪阶层的孩子以贫穷之罪名而获死刑。虽则如此，执政党得到了宗教领袖之中绝大多数的支持，这一群体以教皇为首，令支持社会不公正的迷信之力在全世界范围内扩散。

在教育的前后各个阶段，迷信都造成了灾害级别的影响。某些孩子具备思考的习性，而教育的目标之一就是矫正这一习性。一切不便答复的问题，都回之以“嘘”，甚或予以惩戒。集体情感则用以灌输某种信念，尤其是国族主义信念。资本家、军国主义者和神职人员在教育领域通力合作，因其力量均有赖于情感主义（emotionalism）之流行与批判意见之匮乏。教育则借助人类天性，成功增加并强化了普通人群中的这些倾向。

迷信摧毁教育的另一途径，就是通过影响教师的选择。出于经济考虑，女教师不可结婚；出于道德考虑，她又不可陷入婚外性关系。然而，但凡费心研究过病态心理学的人都知道，旷日持久的童贞通常会对女性造成极大危害，任何健全的社会都应在教师群体中严厉遏止这一现象。种种制约，愈发导致干劲十足而又富于进取的女性拒绝迈入教师行列。这都是迷信禁欲主义久久不散的影响所致。

在中产和上层阶级学校当中，这一情状更形恶劣。校内有礼拜之习，道德方面则由教士负责关照。而教士作为道德教师，几乎必然有两方面是不合格的。他们谴责与人无害的行为，却宽恕害人匪浅的行为。他们都谴责婚前性关系，即使双方相爱，只是尚未确定要不要携手共度此生。他们大都谴责节制生育，而无人谴责丈夫致使妻子因多次孕育而死亡的暴行。我知道有一位颇受欢迎的教士，他的妻子在九年内生了九个孩子。医生告诉他，再生一个她就没命了。次年，她又生了一个，随即撒手人寰。无人谴责；他依旧保有圣职，并且再婚。只要教士依旧宽恕残暴之举，而谴责纯真之喜，由他们来充当年轻人的道德卫士就只会为害。

迷信对于教育的恶劣影响还体现为性知识相关指导的缺失。生理学的主要知识应在青春期到来之前就简单地、自然地传授下去，趁这时候孩子们尚未进入兴奋状态。在青春期，则应教给他们非迷信的性道德基础。应当这样教导少男与少女：除非情投意合，没有什么能赋予性交正当性。这与教会的教导截然相反，教会认为，只要双方已婚配，而男方又盼得一子，性交就是正当的，无论女方有多么不情愿。少男与少女应当学会尊重对方的自由；他们应当明白，没有什么能赋予一个人凌驾于另一个人之上的权利，而嫉妒心与占有欲只会灭杀爱情。他们应当懂得，将另一个生命带来世间乃是大事一桩，孩子必须在健康、环境和父母看护等方面都拥有良好前景时方可降世。但他们也应习得节育之法，以确保孩子只在他们希望的时候到来。最后，他们还须知晓性病之害及其防治之法。性教育倘能照此实施，人类幸福之增长便将不可限量。

人们应当认可，性关系若不涉生育便纯属私事，既无关乎国家，也无碍于邻人。当前，某些不涉生育的性行为受刑法制裁：这便纯属迷信了，因为上述行为除了直接涉事方之外并不影响他人。在涉及生育时，认为令离婚难以操作必然符合孩子的利益，这种想法也是错误的。酗酒、残暴之举和精神错乱都有必要视为离婚的依据，这是为孩子计，同样是为夫妻双方计。当前，人们对通奸的奇特重视相当不合理。显而易见，许多不端行为对婚姻幸福的致命伤害远甚于一次偶然的不忠。男方坚持每年生育一次，这在传统观念里算不上行为不端或残暴之举，实则最为致命。

道德准则不应使本能幸福无法实现。不过，这恰是在一个两性数量极不平等的社会里严格实行一夫一妻制的后果。在此情况下，道德准则自会遭到破坏。然而，当服从准则只能通过社会福祉的大幅衰减来进行，破坏准则却成为比遵守准则更好的选择时，显然是时候改变这些准则了。若不然，许多行事并不危及公众利益的人就会无端面临二选一的局面：要么伪善行事，要么千夫所指。教会并不介意伪善，这可是向其势力奉承的贡品。但在别处，人们已日益将伪善视作一种不应轻易施为的恶。

危害较此神学迷信尤甚者，莫过于国族主义迷信，即迷信个人对祖国的责任而不顾他国。但我并不打算在此讨论太多，只须指出，局限于同胞之间，违背了我们心目中组成美好人生的爱的原则。当然同样违背了觉醒的利己主义，因为就连获胜国也无法从排他性的国族主义中得利。

我们的社会之受累于“罪”这一神学概念，还体现在罪犯的待遇。罪犯是“邪恶的”，“活该”受罚——任何理性的道德都无法支撑这一观点。毋庸置疑，对某些人的所作所为，社会希望能够防止，也确实应当尽一切努力去防止。我们可以举一个最明白的例子：谋杀。显而易见，假如一个社会想要团结为一体，而我们又要享受其间乐事与好处，那便不能允许人们一有冲动就杀人。但这个问题应当用一种纯粹科学的精神来看待。我们应当就这么问：要阻止谋杀，最好的办法是什么？若有两种阻止谋杀的办法同样有效，那么其中对凶手伤害最小的办法就是首选。对凶手的伤害是一种彻头彻尾的可悲，就像外科手术造成的痛一样。或许同样也是必需的，但并不是一桩值得庆贺的事情。人称之为“义愤”的报复情绪，不过是另一形式的残忍。我们加诸罪犯之苦，永远无法以“义愤”之名正当化。假如教育加上好意同样有效，那么这就是首选办法；假如教育加上好意甚至更为有效，那就更应视为首选了。当然，阻止罪行和惩罚罪行是两个不同的问题；至于我们加诸罪犯之苦，其目的或为震慑。假如监狱过于人道，囚犯不须付出即可获得良好教育，人们说不定会为了入狱而犯罪。毋庸置疑，监禁不能比自由更为惬意；但要达成这一结果，最好的办法是将自由变得比当前某些情况下更为惬意。不过，我并不打算在此开启刑罚改革的话题。我只不过想建议大家像对待染疫者一样对待罪犯。两者都是公众威胁，也都必须剥夺其自由，直至他们不再成为威胁。然而，染疫者是同情与怜悯的对象，罪犯却是憎恶的对象。这是相当不理性的。正是因为这一态度区别，我们的监狱祛除犯罪倾向的成效远远不及我们的医院祛除疾病的成效。

## 第四篇　个人救赎与社会救赎

个人主义是传统宗教的缺陷之一，传统宗教相关联的道德同样具有这一缺陷。就传统而言，宗教生活——姑且这么说——乃是灵与神之间的对话。顺从神之意旨，即为美德；此为个人之举，而几乎不必考虑社会情形。新教教派发扬了“皈依得救”（finding salvation）这一观念，但基督教教义中向已有其存在。在历史上的某些阶段，单一灵魂的个人主义自有其价值，然而在现代世界中，我们更需要一种社会性的而非个人性的福利观念。在本篇中，我将论及我们关于美好人生的观念如何受其影响。

基督教兴起于罗马帝国那些与政治权力彻底脱节的人群之中，他们的国族已灭亡，就此融入泯灭个人人格的巨大集合。在基督教时代的前三百年间，皈依基督教的个人无力改变他们所依存的社会或政治体系，尽管他们深知体系之害。在此情境之下，他们很自然地接纳了这样的信念：在这不完美的世界里，个人可臻完美，而美好人生与这世界毫无关联。我这话的意思，比照柏拉图的“理想国”，或许更好理解。当柏拉图想要描述美好人生时，他描述的是一个完整的社会，而非个人；他这是为了定义正义，而正义本质上是一个社会概念。柏拉图对共和制下的公民身份习以为常，并将政治责任视为理所当然的存在。随着希腊式自由的丧失，斯多葛主义崛起了，不同于柏拉图，而更像基督教——关于美好人生，他们秉持一种个人主义概念。

身处伟大的民主制之中，相较于君主专制的罗马，我们应能在自由的雅典找到更为恰当的道德观。在印度，政治环境酷似基督时代的犹地亚，我们看到甘地在传布一种酷似基督所宣扬的道德观，并因此受到罗马总督彼拉多的基督教版传人迫害。然而，较为激进的印度国族主义者不满足于个人救赎：他们想要国族救赎。其间，他们接纳了西方自由民主制的观点。我想指出几个方面，其中这一观点因受基督教影响，尚不具备足够的勇气与自觉，却仍囿于个人救赎的信念。

如我们所想，美好人生需要诸多社会条件，否则无法实现。我们说，美好人生启以爱，导以知。此间所需知识，仅当政府或富人投入其发现与传播之时，方可取得。譬如，癌症的扩散令人惊恐——我们该如何是好？当前，由于知识的匮乏，这一问题无人可解；而且，不通过资助研究，很难获取相关知识。话说回来，科学、历史、文学与艺术方面的知识，应当对一切有意获取的人开放；这就需要当局出面详尽安排了，而改宗换派并不能做到这一点。随后是海外贸易，舍此，则大不列颠有一半居民要忍饥挨饿；如果我们在忍饥挨饿，就不太可能拥有美好人生。种种案例，多说无益。重点在于，在美好人生与不幸人生的一切区别之间，世界乃是一体，那些假装独立过活的人实为寄生虫，无论有意或无意。

个人救赎的理念为早期基督教徒所用，以对其政治上受支配的状态进行自我安慰，一旦我们摆脱了那种关于美好人生的极度狭隘理解，这一理念就不再成立。在正统的基督教观念中，美好人生即美德之人生，美德在于顺从神之意旨，而神之意旨又借良心之声示于个人。整个观念在于：人类受制于外在的专制主义。除美德之外，美好人生还涉及诸多因素，例如智力。而良心是最虚伪不过的向导，因其得自关于幼年所闻训诫的模糊记忆，故此绝不会比持有者的保姆或母亲更高明。要在最完满的意义上实现美好人生，人们必须拥有良好教育、友情、爱情和子女（如有此求），一份足以免于渴求或极度焦虑的收入，良好的健康状况，以及不至于无趣的工作。所有这一切都在不同程度上依赖于社会，并为政治事件所协助或阻碍。美好人生应当在美好社会之中发生，否则无法达成完满。

此即贵族理想的根本缺陷。某些美好事物，诸如艺术、科学、友谊等，在贵族社会诚可蓬勃发展。它们以奴隶制为基础而存在于希腊，也以剥削为基础而存在于我们之中。然而，表现为同情或仁慈的爱，却不能自由存在于贵族社会。贵族阶层总会说服自己：奴隶、无产阶层或有色人种是用下等泥土捏成的，这些人的苦痛不值一提。今时今日，文雅的英国绅士鞭笞非洲人时用力之狠，竟致他们历经数小时不可言说的极度痛苦后身亡。即使这些绅士都受过良好教育，具备艺术修养，兼且善于言辞，我也无法认同他们拥有美好人生。人性之下，同情固有所限，但绝不该是这等程度。在一个倡导民主精神的社会里，也只有疯子才会如此行事。贵族理想所具有的同情之限，恰是其受谴责的缘由。救赎实为一种贵族理想，因为它是一种个人主义的理想。也正是因为这个缘故，个人救赎的理念无论怎么解释或加以扩展，都无法为美好人生下定义。

救赎的另一特征是产于灾变，例如保罗归信①。雪莱的诗篇为这一观念于社会之应用提供了注脚；当所有人改信之时，那一刻降临了，“暴君”纷纷逃窜，而“世界的伟大时代重新开始”。② 或许有人会说，诗人微不足道，其观点无关紧要。但

① 保罗起初认为耶稣是违背犹太教传统信仰的异端。后来他在往大马色迫害门徒途中受日光照射而目盲，其间听到耶稣的声音，受到启发并重获光明，决定改信基督，遂成为后世所知的外邦人使徒。详见《圣经·使徒行传》。——译注

② 语出雪莱长篇诗剧《希腊》(*Hellas*)，49/1060 行。江枫译文参见《雪莱全集》，河北教育出版社，2000 年，第 4 卷，第 72 页。——译注

我确信，大部分革命领袖的观点与雪莱所持者极度相似。他们以为，一切苦难、残暴与堕落都源自暴君、神父、资本家或德国人，一旦推翻这些罪魁祸首，人心就会为之一变，我们也从此过上了幸福生活。只因心怀此念，他们一向乐于“以战止战”。那些遭遇失败或死亡的人相对而言还算幸运；那些不幸取胜的人在他们的辉煌希望惨遭破灭之后，反而陷入愤世嫉俗或绝望的深渊。这些希望的终极根源，正是将灾变改信视为救赎之道的基督教义。

我不愿妄言革命绝无必要，唯愿指出革命并非通往千禧盛世的捷径。无论在个人层面或社会层面，都不存在通往美好人生的捷径。要建设美好人生，我们必须在智力、自控和同情方面都有所积累。这是一个数量问题，涉及逐步改进、早期训练和教育实验。盖因急躁不耐，才会相信骤然改进有可能发生。真正可能发生的逐步改进及其得以实现的方法，是未来或可解决的问题。但我们眼下也并非无话可说。在尾声中，我将对此试述一二。

# 第五篇　科学与幸福

道德家意在改进人类行为。不得不称其雄心可嘉，因为他们的行为大都十分不堪。然而，不管是道德家所欲求的具体改进，还是他用以实现改进的方法，我都无法为之称颂。他台面上的方法是道德说教，真正的方法（如果他属于天主教派）则是经济赏罚制。前者带来的影响并不长久，也不重要；自萨沃纳罗拉[①]以降，宗教复兴派带来的影响总是转瞬即逝。后者——赏罚——则确有成效。例如，赏罚制令男人情愿和娼妓春风一度而不肯养情妇，因为需要采取最隐蔽的方法。他们由此而令这一风险极高的行业得以运转，性病为之流行。这并非

① 萨沃纳罗拉（Girolamo Savonarola，1452—1498），意大利多明我会修士，1494—1498年任佛罗伦萨的精神和世俗领袖。他反对宗教腐败、世俗享乐和商业经营，焚烧了文艺复兴期间的大量艺术品与书籍，以严厉的布道著称。——译注

道德家所欲求者，但他过于缺乏科学头脑，竟未察觉这正是他实际造成的后果。

要取代这种不科学的布道加贿赂大法，还有没有更好的路可走？我想是有的。

人类行动之所以造成危害，若非源自无知，就是出于恶欲。从社会角度来看，“恶”欲可定义为意在阻挠他人欲求的欲求，确切而言，即其所阻挠的欲求多于其所助力的欲求。源自无知的危害无须细述；此间所需，莫过于更多的知识，故此，改进之法在于更多的研究和更多的教育。出于恶欲的危害则更为棘手。

凡人男女身上活跃着某种程度的恶意，包括对特定敌人的特定敌意，以及对他人的幸灾乐祸。人们常以言辞精心将其掩饰，传统道德约有半数是在为其涂脂傅粉。然而，道德家若要实现改进我们人类行动的目标，就不得不面对这一点。这一点处处可见，不遗巨细：见于人们一再重复并相信丑闻的欢欣之态，见于明知善待罪犯对其改造更有成效却仍加以虐待之举，见于全体白人对黑人令人发指的野蛮行为，见于一战期间老太太与教士们指点年轻人参军义务的热忱。就连儿童也可能成为恣意暴行的对象：大卫·考坡菲和奥立弗·退斯特绝非凭空想象。这种活跃的恶意乃是人性之至恶，假如这个世界想变得更幸福，最需要改变的就是这一点。这一原因与战争之间的牵连，或许比所有经济、政治原因加在一起还要多。

有了防范恶意这一问题，我们该如何应对？首先，让我们理解其来由。我以为，其中一部分是社会原因，一部分是心理原因。这个世界从过去到现在都立足于生死攸关的竞争；一战期间的关键问题在于，是德国儿童还是协约国儿童应当死于饥渴。（抛开双方的恶意，没有任何理由表明双方不能同生。）大多数人打心底里怀有一种对毁灭的深深恐惧；尤其是那些拖儿带女的人。富人生恐布尔什维克会没收他们的资产；穷人生恐失去工作或健康身体。所有人都陷入了对“安全感”的狂热追求，想象着唯有征服潜在敌人才能获得这种安全感。恰恰是在惊恐之中，暴行蔓延，愈演愈烈。各地反动派都诉诸恐惧：在英格兰，是对布尔什维主义的恐惧；在法国，是对德国的恐惧；在德国，是对法国的恐惧。这些诉求的唯一结果就是，他们所欲保护的对象反而面临更大的危险。

因此，具备科学头脑的道德家应将战胜恐惧列为首要关注之一。为此，可从以下两点着手：一方面增强安全，一方面培育勇气。我在这里提及的恐惧是一种非理性情感，而不是对于潜在灾祸的理性预见。当剧院着火时，理性的人和惊恐的人一样明明白白地预见了灾难后果，但理性的人采取了有可能减灾的方法，惊恐的人反而加剧了灾难后果。一九一四年以来的欧洲，就像着火的剧院中一名惊恐的观众；此时需要镇定、权威的指挥，引导大家有序逃生，以免将彼此踩踏成泥。维多利亚时代虽然空话连篇，却是迅猛发展的时期，因为此间主宰乃是希望，而非恐惧。如欲重新获得发展，我们必须让希望做回主宰。

凡可增强普遍安全的一切，往往也能削弱暴行。这不仅适用于防止战争，无论是通过国际联盟[①]或其他；也适用于通过医药、保健与公共卫生方面的改进来改善健康；更适用于一切减缓恐怖的方法，这恐怖潜藏在人类心灵深处，每当他们入眠时便成了梦魇。但若我们努力让一部分人类获得安全，却要以另一部分人类为代价——法国人以德国人为代价，资本家以工薪阶层为代价，白种人以黄种人为代价，诸如此类——那就是徒劳无益了。这种方法只会在优势群体中平添恐怖，生怕单单愤恨会令受压迫者揭竿而起。唯有正义能赋予安全；而我所谓"正义"，指的是承认全体人类的平等要求。

不过，除了旨在带来安全的社会变革之外，还有另一种更直接的削弱恐惧之法，那就是旨在增添勇气的政权。鉴于勇气在战场上的重要性，人们早就发现了增添勇气的办法，即通过教育和饮食——例如，吃人肉一度被视为有效之法。然而，军事上的勇气总是统治集团的特权：斯巴达人比奴隶拥有更多，大英军官比印度士兵拥有更多，男人比女人拥有更多，依此类推。几百年来，勇气一向被视为贵族的特权。统治集团每添一

① 国际联盟（League of Nations），简称国联，成立于 1920 年巴黎和会召开后。这是世界上第一个以维护世界和平为主要任务的国际组织，在本书写作的 1920 年代有显著功绩，但终未阻止二战爆发。1946 年为联合国所取代。——译注

分勇气，受压迫者肩上就要承担多一道重负，压迫者据以产生恐惧的根基便再添一分，引起暴行的理由也就无从削弱了。勇气必须民主化，方可使人之为人。

在很大程度上，通过近期发生的事件，勇气已经开始民主化了。女性参政论者表明她们拥有的勇气不输最英勇的男人；这一表现对她们赢得投票至关重要。一战中的普通士兵所需的勇气并不亚于一名上校或中尉，更是远远超过一名将军；这与他在退伍后不须应召有很大关系。自诩为无产阶级捍卫者的布尔什维克也不缺乏勇气，无论他们在其他方面声名如何；这已为其革命前的表现所证明。在武士阶层一度独享尚武精神的日本，正是征兵制向全体男性提出了对勇气的需求。由此可见，过去半个世纪以来，所有大国都付出了诸多努力，以使勇气不再为贵族独享：如若不然，民主所面临的危险就会远超当下。

但战斗中的勇气绝非其唯一形式，甚至称不上最重要的形式。也有面对贫困的勇气、面对嘲笑的勇气和面对己方敌意的勇气。可叹便是最勇敢的士兵，也往往付之阙如。更不要说在面对危险时保持平静与理性的思考、在惊慌引发的恐惧或愤怒之下控制冲动的勇气。以上这些，自可通过教育的助力取得。而有了良好的健康、强壮的体格和充足的营养，加上生命基本冲动的自由宣泄，各种形式的勇气也会更易授予。通过比较猫与兔的血液，或可找到勇气在生理上的来源。对于增进我们的勇气，科学可为之事几无止境，例如冒险经历、锻炼健身与合理饮食。然而，我们上流社会之子大都享有的这一切，至今仍多为与财富挂钩的特权。目前，在社会较贫困阶层之中激发的勇气只是听令而行的勇气，尚不具备主动性与领导力。当那些造就领导力的品质遍及各人，领导者与追随者之分不再存在，民主也就终将实现。

不过，恐惧并非恶意的唯一来源；嫉恨与幻灭同样有所贡献。众所周知，瘸子与罗锅的嫉恨之心乃是怨艾之源，但除此之外，其他不幸也能造成类似后果。性受挫的男女很容易满怀嫉恨；这往往表现为对幸运者的道德诋毁。革命运动有很大一部分驱动力源自对富人的嫉恨。妒忌当然也是嫉恨的一种特殊形式——对爱的嫉恨。[①] 老年人常常嫉恨青年人，这时他们往往会虐待对方。

就我所知，目前还没有什么办法可以解决嫉恨，除了让嫉恨者的人生美满丰富起来，并在青年人之中倡导集体事业而非竞争的观念。形式最为恶劣的嫉恨来自那些在婚姻、亲子或职业方面未能称心如意的人。就大多数案例而言，更好的社会制度可以避免此类不幸。然而，我们必须承认，嫉恨很可能会有所残留。史上多有此例，将军们互相妒忌，宁可战败也不愿让

① 妒忌（jealousy）与嫉恨（envy）之辨：两词在英文中区别明显，jealousy 是因对方可能夺去自己所欲求或已有之优势而产生的猜忌心理，在三角关系中表现为占有欲，俗称“吃醋”；envy 则是看到对方拥有高于自己的优势时产生的屈辱与渴望。——译注

对方收获声名。同属一党的两名政客，或同属一派的两名艺术家，几乎势必互相妒忌。在此类案例中似乎无路可走，只能尽量保证各位竞争者无法伤害彼此，唯有凭借巨大优势取胜。艺术家的妒忌往往为害甚微，因为既然他没有打算毁掉对手的作品，唯一有效的满足之法就是画出更好的作品。当嫉恨无法避免时，应通过这一刺激来促进自身的努力，而不是去挫败对手的努力。

在增进人类幸福这一方面，科学的可能性并不局限在削弱人性中趋于两败俱伤的部分，即我们据以称为“恶”的部分。在增进积极美德这一方面，科学可为之事几无止境。健康状况已经获得巨大改善；虽有些恋旧者为之唱哀歌，不管和十八世纪哪个阶层、哪个国族相比，我们总是寿命更长、病痛更少。只要对我们已掌握的知识稍稍多加应用，我们或许会比现在健康得多。而未来的发现很可能使这一进程大幅加速。

目前，还是自然科学对我们的生活影响最广，但在未来，生理学与心理学带来的影响很可能远在其上。等我们发现生理条件是如何决定了性格，要是我们愿意，就能打造出更多我们所钦慕的那一类人。智力、艺能、仁慈——所有这一切，无疑均可通过科学增进。只要人类肯善用科学，那么，在打造更美好的世界这一方面，可为之事或无止境。我曾在别处阐明我的恐惧，担心人类无法对他们取自科学的力量善加利用。[①] 眼下，我所考虑的是人类选择向善时所能为之善，而非人类是否情愿选择为害这一问题。

对科学在人类生活中的应用，存在那么一种态度，令我有所共鸣，但作为结论又不敢苟同。那就是人们对一切“不自然的”事物心怀忧惧的态度。卢梭自是这一观点在欧洲最大的倡导者。在亚洲，老子对这一观点的阐述甚至更令人信服，而且还早了两千四百年。我认为，在对“自然”的钦慕中，真理与谬误难解难分，重要的是对此进行厘清。首先，何为“自然的”？略而言之，即论者幼年时所惯见的一切。老子反对的道路舟车[②]，大概都是在他出生的村子里见不到的东西。卢梭习惯了这些东西，便不觉其有违自然。但若他活到铁路问世的年代，无疑也会大加抨击。衣服和烹饪的历史过于悠久，大部分自然的信徒都不至于横加指责，即便他们都反对新式样。有人视节制生育为邪恶之举，却能容忍禁欲之行，因为前者是一种新出现的悖逆自然，后者则由来已久。如此种种，足见自然鼓吹者之前后矛盾，令人不由视其为保守分子。

即便如此，他们并非一无可取之处。以维生素为例，其发现引得“自然的”食物突然回潮。然而，鱼肝油和电光似乎也

① 参见拙作《伊卡洛斯：科学的未来》。

② 应指《道德经》谈及“小国寡民”理想时所云“使民重死，而不远徙。虽有舟舆，无所乘之……民至老死，不相往来”。——译注

能提供维生素，这可不属于人类“自然的”饮食。此例可证，无知之下，对自然做出新的背离可能带来无法预料的危害；而当人们渐渐了解这一危害之后，往往很快就会以新的人造物来弥补。至于我们的物质环境与我们满足欲求的物质手段，“自然”主义除了证明在采用新对策时应当谨慎试验之外，我不认为还有什么别的意义。譬如说，衣服有违自然，且要保证它们不致病，还须佐以另一种不自然措施：洗涤。然而，两相叠加，就能让我们比一无所有的野人更健康。

在人类欲求这一方面，“自然”还有更多可取之处。将某种生活强加给男女儿童而令其最强烈的冲动受挫，不仅残酷，而且危险；在此意义上，给定某些附带条件，依照“自然”去生活就是值得嘉许的。论人为者莫过于地铁，但儿童去搭乘地铁对其天性并无折损；相反，几乎所有儿童都会觉得这一体验再愉快不过了。在同等条件下，能满足普通人欲求的人为之物就是好的。不过，受权威与经济需求所迫而选择的人为生活方式就不可取了。毋庸置疑，眼下这样的生活方式在某种程度上是必要的；轮船少了司炉，远洋航行就会寸步难行。但此类需求未免令人遗憾，我们也应设法将其免除。一定的工作量并不会引发抱怨；实际上，这多半比饱食终日、无所事事更令人幸福。然而，眼下人们必须完成的工作量以及工种，都可谓惨淡之至：那些终其一生无法摆脱的日常事务，尤为不堪。人生不可管制太严，或过于井井有条；我们的冲动只要不是确确实实对他人造成毁灭或伤害，就该在可能的情况下任其自由宣泄；要给冒险留些空间。我们应当遵从人类天性，因为我们的幸福须从我们的冲动和欲求中去酝酿。给人某些抽象意义上的“好”东西并没有用；假如我们要带来更多幸福，就必须给予某些他们所欲求或所需要的东西。假以时日，科学或可学会塑造我们的欲求，令其自此不再与他人的欲求产生冲突；与现在相比，到那时我们将能够满足我们的欲求中的更大多数。在此并仅仅在此意义上，我们的欲求就会变得“更好”。孤立状态下的单一欲求无谓更好或更坏；但如果有一系列欲求能够同时获得满足，而另一系列欲求彼此之间互不调和，那么前者就比后者更好。这就是爱之所以比恨更好的缘故。

遵从物质自然是愚蠢之举；应以使之尽最大可能服务于人类目的为考量，对物质自然进行研究，但在伦理意义上，它始终无谓好坏善恶。在物质自然与人类相会之处，譬如考虑人口问题时，不必束手臣服，兀自相信唯有通过战争、疫病和饥荒才能解决过度生育。神学家们宣称：就此而言，将科学应用于问题的物质一面乃是恶行；我们必须（他们如是说）将道德应用于人性一面，实施节欲。且不说就连神学家本人都知道这一建议无人采纳，运用物质手段避孕以解决人口问题又何以成为恶行呢？对此能给出的答案莫不来自陈旧教条。显而易见，神学家所宣扬的悖逆自然，至少并不亚于节制生育。神学家选择的悖逆自然，一旦成功实施，便将招致不幸、嫉恨与迫害倾向，并往往伴随疯狂。而我宁肯选择与蒸汽机甚或打雨伞同类的“悖逆”自然。由此可见，我们应遵循“自然”这一原则的应用是何等含混不清、捉摸不定。

自然，甚或人类本性，渐渐不再是一种绝对基准，而将日益成为科学操作所塑造的模样。只要人们愿意，科学就能通过给予知识、自控以及促进和谐而非冲突的品性，使我们的孙辈享有美好人生。当前科学教给我们子辈的是如何自相残杀，因为许多科学工作者情愿牺牲人类的未来，换自己一时的成功。然而，当人类得以像他们掌控外在世界那样掌控自我情感之时，这一阶段便告终结。那时，我们也终将收获属于我们的自由。

# Contents

# Preface To The Routledge Classics Edition

Fifty years after reading Bertrand Russell for the first time, I read him today with mixed feelings. In the middle 1950s, his *History of Western Philosophy* was a treat to teenage schoolboys bored to death with the slog of O Level. It gave us all the weapons we needed to torment the school chaplain when he tried to explain to agnostic teenagers Aquinas's Five Ways to the knowledge of God's existence. *Why I am not a Christian* was an even more valuable weapon against authority. My housemaster's belief that Russell's four marriages discredited his views on sex,

God and nuclear warfare only confirmed my view that most holders of authority were bigoted, illogical and not to be taken seriously.

I have not wholly changed my mind. Russell's four marriages are irrelevant to his views on sex, God and nuclear warfare; I now think that his marital difficulties should have made him more wary about making the pursuit of happiness look *easy*, but his ideas about what the good life is wear well. He had many vices as a critic of views he disliked, and his practice was at odds with his professed principle of taking on one's opponents at their strongest points rather than their weakest. In those ways, he was less admirable than John Stuart Mill. On the other hand, he was, and is, much more fun. In particular, he wrote wonderfully; even the articles he turned out for the Hearst newspapers at fifty dollars a pop, in order to support Beacon Hill, the school that he and his second wife had created, are not only quick and clever, but thought-provoking too. If Britain took literacy seriously, teenagers would be given Russell as a model essayist.

During the First World War Russell realized that he had an extraordinary talent for lecturing to lay audiences. He was deeply opposed to the war and, as a member of the Union for Democratic Control early in the war and later as a leading figure in the No-Conscription Fellowship, he worked unceasingly to bring the war to an early end, to persuade the United States to remain neutral, and to protect conscientious objectors from abuse at the hand of the tribunals that heard their case for exemption, and from ill-treatment in prison or the army, if they ended up there. These activities cost him his lecturership at Trinity College, Cambridge, but they brought him into a new world, too.

In addition to the innumerable meetings aimed directly at bringing an end to the war and saving objectors from conscription, Russell gave a strikingly successful series of lectures on *The Principles of Social Reconstruction*. To the extent that he had a single political philosophy, it was contained in the short book that the lectures became. Much that is taken for granted in *What I Believe* is argued for at some length in *The Principles of Social Reconstruction*. Three crucial premises are worth bringing into the light.

Russell's view of human behaviour was rooted in the empiricist tradition that held that *desire* propels all action, and that the role of reason is to tell us *how* to achieve what we are after, not *what* we should be after in the first place. Or, as Hume put it with the sharpness that Russell relished, 'reason is and ought to be the slave of the passions'. This was not an argument for 'impulsiveness' in the ordinary sense: Russell believed that we should think very hard about what we are up to, and he wanted more, and more scientifically informed, reflection on what we ought to do with our lives. It was an argument for trying to understand what it is that we do really want. Russell's views about the basis of our desires went farther than that. He was well acquainted with the work of W. H. Rivers, the psychiatrist who treated Siegfried Sassoon — and many others — for shell shock, and who was one of the first people in England to take the measure of Freud. Rivers thought Freud exaggerated his insights, but had no doubt that we are all much more at the mercy of hidden impulses than we like to think. So did Russell.

In particular, Russell came close to believing that human beings were instinctively impelled to destruction for its own sake, something that Freud's account of the 'death wish' also suggests. It was so obvious to him that war between nation states was unnecessary, and therefore deeply stupid, that he found it hard to believe that anything could explain it other than a passion for destruction and a desire by the combatants to inflict suffering on others at no matter what price in suffering for themselves. To believe anything so nihilistic, however, would have made Russell's pacifism futile. If we are determined to destroy ourselves for no good reasorn, the only interesting question is how long it will be before we find the technology to wipe ourselves out completely. Russell was always ready for rhetorical purposes to represent his opponents as imbued with a passion to commit mass murder and mass suicide, but in his more analytical moments, he proposed a different and more elaborate view.

This view was the second premise of his politics. He argued in *Principles* that there are two kinds of impulse; the *possessive* impulse seeks exclusive ownership of whatever it lights on, and leads us to compete with each other, while the *creative* impulse leads us to look for things that can be had by one person without anyone else being any the worse for it. If German scientists discover dazzling new theorems in physics, it leaves no fewer dazzling new theorems to be discovered by French and British scientists, whereas the German seizure of South West Africa leaves so much the less territory for the French and British, to say nothing of the original inhabitants. If possessiveness gets attached to national glory, and national glory is then conceived as requiring the humiliation of other nations, we have the recipe for endless wars. Peace and happiness can only be secured by encouraging the creative instincts and diverting the possessive instincts to useful or at any rate harmless ends.

Third, then, come the ethics that Russell found it in

himself to preach. As a matter of logic in the narrowest sense, Russell's ethics owe nothing to his larger philosophical views. This is a point he made for himself innumerable times. Strictly, he said, there could be no philosophical defence of any particular morality; philosophy is concerned with issues in which truth is at stake. Moral judgement is exhortation, encouragement, reproach — the expression of attitudes in favour of or hostile to whatever action, or character trait might be under discussion. 'Murder is evil' does not state a property of murder; it denounces murder. Moral philosophy is not philosophy at all. This was a dramatic way to make a familiar point. Russell often offered analyses of the logic of moral utterances that are unequivocally philosophical in the modern sense. It is, however, easy to see what drove Russell. For a long time, he held that even the most abstract branches of philosophy — logic and the foundations of mathematics included — are concerned to show the world as it really is. Morality's concern is with how the world should be rather than with how it is.

Given all that, Russell's ethical theory is unsurprising. Our impulses *in themselves* are neither good nor bad; they are brute facts. They are good and bad according to the way they assist or frustrate other impulses, either our own or those of other people. My desire to drink myself silly is just a desire, but it is at odds with my desire to wake up without a hangover; it is at odds with your desire to travel the roads safely, as well as with my employer's desire to have a coherent receptionist in the front office. Drinking oneself silly is at best imprudent and in many circumstances wicked. The wish to be helpful and co-operative on the other hand, assists others to realize their goals and will not impede my other desires. We therefore call benevolence, helpfulness and kindness good. Our standards of prudent and morally acceptable behaviour rest on our assessment of what Russell later called the 'compossibility' of desire. We should cultivate those desires that assist in the satisfaction of desires and eliminate those that frustrate them.

The connection with Russell's account of the creative instincts, and his hatred of the war hardly needs labouring.

Nor does the fact that couching his account of ethics in terms of desire-satisfaction seems to provide the basis for a secular, naturalistic, and hedonistic moral theory. It is arguable that if Russell had been consistent, this is what he would have offered his readers. In fact, he did not; what emerged was secular and naturalistic, but not (mostly) a defence of hedonism. Very much like his godfather, John Stuart Mill, Russell stood up for high ideals that are only loosely connected to the pursuit of happiness in any everyday sense — courage, for instance, the love of truth, and a non-instrumental concern for the natural world among them. Rightly or wrongly, Russell agreed with Mill that Socrates dissatisfied is a better man than the fool satisfied. *What I Believe* defends the disinterested pursuit of the truth as one element in the good life, and Russell's most passionate complaint against religion is that it is a *cowardly* response to the bleakness of the universe.

*What I Believe* appeared in a series of very short books — the publishers described them as 'Pamphlets' — called 'Today and Tomorrow'. They were very short books on very large subjects: 'the future of Women, War, Population, Science, Machines, Morals, Drama, Poetry, Art, Music, Sex, etc.' Dora Russell wrote *Hypatia* in defence of women's liberation and Russell wrote two pamphlets in the series, of which *What I Believe* was the second. J. B. S. Haldane's *Daedalus*, had offered an optimistic view of what science would do for humanity in the future; Russell riposted with *Icarus*, to point out that Daedalus's son learned how to fly, but not how to fly intelligently. Since science as the fruit of rational inquiry into the world could only tell us *how* to achieve our goals, it was all too likely that the most impressive result of scientific advance would be to turn warfare into global massacre. If we avoided that fate, we would either find ourselves bored to death as large scale bureaucracies took over the management of the world, or be turned into the docile creatures imagined in Huxley's *Brave New World* — a book that was probably inspired by Russell's *Icarus* — genetically engineered to fit into our social roles, and fed drugs that would achieve whatever eugenics had not.

Because Russell was one of the founders of the Campaign for Nuclear Disarmament, and a prolific writer on the horrors of nuclear warfare, it is easy to forget that his fears for the future of humanity were not first aroused by nuclear weapons, but by the industrialized warfare of the First World War, and then by the advent of the long-range bomber in the 1930s. *Icarus* was mordant in its wit, savagely unfair in its characterization of almost all holders of power as wicked and reckless, and deeply pessimistic about the prospects of the human race. Not for the last time did Russell express the view that it might be a good thing for humanity to exterminate itself, since it made such a mess of existence.

*What I Believe* was avowedly intended to redress the balance. It is so lucid and so amusing that explaining its contents to a reader about to have the pleasure of reading Russell for themselves seems foolish. What may be more helpful is to say a little about Russell's characteristic stance on matters of religion, and about the decidedly upbeat conclusion of *What I Believe*, in which the productive rather than the destructive possibilities of science are broached as a counter to the gloom of *Icarus*.

There are two sorts of atheist — Russell called himself an agnostic to indicate that it was not *impossible* that there should be some sort of God, but he was perfectly certain that God did not exist, and atheist seems more apt. The position of the first sort of atheist is sometimes paraphrased as 'there is no God, and I hate him'; he or she wishes that there was a God, in order to have someone to complain at about the absurdity of the universe. Leonard Woolf once remarked that he would like to question God about the design of the human digestive system, the plumbing of which seemed peculiarly inept. The second sort of atheist is more bored than outraged; he or she cannot see what purpose is served by inventing stories about gods, spirits, or whatever supernatural entities you care to name; they add nothing to our understanding of the world, and bring with them intellectual clutter and grounds for mutual persecution when our species hardly needs to be encouraged in its incoherence and violence. One can be both sorts, but it is rhetorically awkward to be both at once.

Russell was as often the first sort of atheist as the second, but *What I Believe* is mostly written from this second point of view. All the same, it is the first sort of atheism that supplies much of the emotional force even of this essay. Atheists who cannot see why anyone would bother to invent unbelievable stories about the origins of the universe and how we are supposed to behave, might be expected to say nothing on the subject and to devote themselves to other matters. Russell rarely passed up an opportunity to speak unkindly about the devout — and was repaid in kind.

The obvious explanation is that Russell was at least half convinced that human existence was a miserable business; life could have been wonderful, but very largely was not. It was therefore intolerable to think that some being might deliberately have created a world in which we suffer constant anxiety, die of painful diseases when we do not die of violence, and suffer vastly more acute pains from heartbreak and disappointment than the pleasures of love and realized ambition can justify. If there were a God, he, she, it, or they should be tried for crimes against humanity. The devout are guilty of praising wickedness, either because they are too cowardly to face the fact that God is a criminal, or because they have a perverted sense of morality and really believe that might makes right.

The atheism of *What I Believe* is of the less inflamed, second kind. What there is to be known about the world is what science reveals, and there is no good reason to suppose either that we are immortal, or that some ghostly clockmaker stands behind the machinery of the universe. Nonetheless, some sharp complaints are levelled at the role of religion in ethics and politics. Russell particularly seizes the occasion to denounce the religious for advocating birth control by war and famine while trying to prevent birth control using contraception as advocated by Margaret Sanger and others at the time. Russell, of course, took a delight in enraging the devout by arguments such as these. Many of his readers deplore his frequent unfairness, but there was a serious point behind his rhetorical tactics.

It is this: many religions — Christianity particularly — pay an obsessive attention to matters of sexual conduct. Instead of asking what would allow people to lead tolerably happy lives, bring up enough, but not too many, healthy, happy and decently educated children, Christians, in Russell's view, spend their time making it harder rather than easier to think about such things calmly. Looking at the opponents of abortion in the United States almost eighty years later, it is easy to sympathize with Russell. The godly got their revenge on Russell in 1940, when a New York court overturned his appointment at City College on the grounds that he taught 'immorality'. *What I Believe* was part of the evidence his enemies appealed to.

At least one of Russell's objections to religiously based moralities would apply to more than those moralities which are based on religion, narrowly defined. Russell was hostile to all forms of ethics based on rules. Rightly enough, Russell thought morality plays a very small part in life. Nobody looks up the rules about parental duty when caring for a sick child, for instance; they are motivated by love — or not — and in either event morality plays no role. If they lack proper affection, they will not be moralized into it, and if they feel it, the moral standpoint is redundant. Russell was especially hostile to the thought that morality consists of rules laid down by some authority, whether God or the superego. Rules are inflexible, and the one thing Russell was sure of was that intelligent thought about our conduct must have a flexibility that matched the changeability of events.

Finally, then, the role of science in all this. In *What I Believe*, Russell said firmly that we should not 'respect' nature but learn how nature works so as to turn nature's powers to useful human ends. There are two things to be said about this. First, as we have seen, Russell was in two minds about whether humanity had the sense to use science for good ends rather than bad; the tendency in *Icarus* is to dwell on the probability that we shall misuse science, but in *What I Believe* it is to exhort us to use it for good ends. Secondly, Russell relies very heavily on the contrast between religion and morality conceived as inflexible rules that lack any rational basis or gratify the human taste for cruelty, and science conceived as the piecemeal understanding of what causes what on the other. The scientific attitude is what he wants to foster.

He was not always eager to tell his readers not to respect nature. Forty years later he commented bitterly on the eagerness of mankind to defile the heavens by putting into orbit satellites that would launch nuclear warheads at the enemy, and he accused the American pragmatist John Dewey of 'impiety' in suggesting that nature was somehow infused with human purpose. This is not a simple contradiction. At no time did Russell think that nature provided a moral standard or was itself a source of norms for our conduct; when he denounces 'respect in *What I Believe*, that is the point he is making. At the same time he always found the vast emptiness of the universe deeply moving — terrifying and consoling at the same time. That emotion has led many readers to decide that Russell was despite himself a deeply religious thinker. If so, he was one of many religious thinkers who have found all actual religions repulsively inadequate to the sentiments they purport to express.

2003 ALAN RYAN

# Preface

In this little book, I have tried to say what I think of man's place in the universe, and of his possibilities in the way of achieving the good life. In *Icarus* I expressed my fears; in the following pages I have expressed my hopes. The inconsistency is only apparent. Except in astronomy, mankind have not achieved the art of predicting the future; in human affairs, we can see that there are forces making for happiness, and forces making for misery. We do not know which will prevail, but to act wisely we must be aware of both.

*January*, 1st 1925 B. R.

# 1

# NATURE AND MAN

Man is a part of Nature, not something contrasted with Nature. His thoughts and his bodily movements follow the same laws that describe the motions of stars and atoms. The physical world is large compared with Man — larger than it was thought to be in Dante's time, but not so large as it seemed a hundred years ago. Both upward and downward, both in the large and in the small, science seems to be reaching limits. It is thought that the universe is of finite extent in space, and that light could travel round it in a few hundred millions of years. It is thought matter consists of electrons and protons, which are of finite size and of which there are only a finite number in the world. Probably their changes are not continuous, as used to be thought, but proceed by jerks, which are never smaller than a certain minimum jerk. The laws of these changes can apparently be summed up in a small number of very general principles, which determine the past and the future of the world when any small section of its history is known.

Physical science is thus approaching the stage when it will be complete, and therefore uninteresting. Given the laws governing the motions of electrons and protons, the rest is merely geography — a collection of particular facts telling their distribution throughout some portion of the world's history. The total number of facts of geography required to determine the world's history is probably finite; theoretically they could all be written down in a big book to be kept at Somerset House with a calculating machine attached which, by turning a handle, would enable the inquirer to find out the facts at other times than those recorded. It is difficult to imagine anything less interesting or more different from the passionate delights of incomplete discovery. It is like climbing a high mountain and finding nothing at the top except a restaurant where they sell ginger beer, surrounded by fog but equipped with wireless. Perhaps in the times of Ahmes the multiplication table was exciting.

Of this physical world, uninteresting in itself, Man is a part. His body, like other matter, is composed of electrons and protons, which, so far as we know, obey the same laws as those not forming part of animals or plants. There are some who maintain that physiology can never be reduced to physics, but their arguments are not very convincing and it seems prudent to suppose that they are mistaken. What we call our 'thoughts' seem to depend upon the organisation of tracks in the brain in the same sort of way in which journeys depend upon roads and railways. The energy used in thinking seems to have a chemical origin; for instance, a deficiency of iodine will turn a clever man into an idiot. Mental phenomena seem to be bound up with material structure. If this be so, we cannot suppose that a solitary electron or proton can 'think'; we might as well expect a solitary individual to play a football match. We also cannot suppose that an individual's thinking survives bodily death, since that destroys the organisation of the brain, and dissipates the energy which utilised the brain tracks.

God and immortality, the central dogmas of the Christian religion, find no support in science. It cannot be said that either doctrine is essential to religion, since neither is found in Buddhism. (With regard to immortality, this statement in an unqualified form might be misleading, but it is correct in the last analysis.) But we in the West have come to think of them as the irreducible minimum of theology. No doubt people will continue to entertain these beliefs, because they are pleasant, just as it is pleasant to think ourselves virtuous and our enemies wicked. But for my part I cannot see any ground for either. I do not pretend to be able to prove that there is no God. I equally cannot prove that Satan is a fiction. The

Christian God may exist; so may the Gods of Olympus, or of ancient Egypt, or of Babylon. But no one of these hypotheses is more probable than any other: they lie outside the region of even probable knowledge, and therefore there is no reason to consider any of them. I shall not enlarge upon this question, as I have dealt with it elsewhere. ①

The question of personal immortality stands on a somewhat different footing. Here evidence either way is possible. Persons are part of the everyday world with which science is concerned, and the conditions which determine their existence are discoverable. A drop of water is not immortal; it can be resolved into oxygen and hydrogen. If, therefore, a drop of water were to maintain that it had a quality of aqueousness which would survive its dissolution we should be inclined to be sceptical. In like manner we know that the brain is not immortal, and that the organised energy of a living body becomes, as it were,

---

① See my *Philosophy of Leibniz*, Chapter XV.

demobilised at death, and therefore not available for collective action. All the evidence goes to show that what we regard as our mental life is bound up with brain structure and organised bodily energy. Therefore it is rational to suppose that mental life ceases when bodily life ceases. The argument is only one of probability, but it is as strong as those upon which most scientific conclusions are based.

There are various grounds upon which this conclusion might be attacked. Psychical research professes to have actual scientific evidence of survival, and undoubtedly its procedure is, in principle, scientifically correct. Evidence of this sort might be so overwhelming that no one with a scientific temper could reject it. The weight to be attached to the evidence, however, must depend upon the antecedent probability of the hypothesis of survival. There are always different ways of accounting for any set of phenomena and of these we should prefer the one which is antecedentally least improbable. Those who already think it likely that we survive death will be ready to view this theory as the best explanation of psychical phenomena. Those who, on other grounds, regard this theory as implausible will seek for other explanations. For my part, I consider the evidence so far adduced by psychical research in favour of survival much weaker than the physiological evidence on the other side. But I fully admit that it might at any moment become stronger, and in that case it would be unscientific to disbelieve in survival.

Survival of bodily death is, however, a different matter from immortality: it may only mean a postponement of psychical death. It is immortality that men desire to believe in. Believers in immortality will object to physiological arguments, such as I have been using, on the ground that soul and body are totally disparate, and that the soul is something quite other than its empirical manifestations through our bodily organs. I believe this to be a metaphysical superstition. Mind and matter alike are for certain purposes convenient terms, but are not ultimate realities. Electrons and protons, like the soul, are logical fictions; each is really a history, a series of events, not a single persistent entity. In the case of the soul, this is obvious from the facts of growth. Whoever considers conception, gestation, and infancy cannot seriously believe that the soul in any indivisible something, perfect and complete throughout this process. It is evident that it grows like the body, and that it derives both from the spermatozoon and from the ovum, so that it cannot be indivisible. This is not materialism: it is merely the recognition that everything interesting is a matter of organisation, not of primal substance.

Metaphysicians have advanced innumerable arguments to prove that the soul must be immortal. There is one simple test by which all these arguments can be demolished. They all prove equally that the soul must pervade all space. But as we are not so anxious to be fat as to live long, none of the metaphysicians in question have ever noticed this application of their reasonings. This is an instance of the amazing power of desire in blinding even very able men to fallacies which would otherwise be obvious at once. If we were not afraid of death, I do not believe that the idea of immortality would ever have arisen.

Fear is the basis of religious dogma, as of so much else in human life. Fear of human beings, individually or collectively, dominates much of our social life, but it is fear of nature that gives rise to religion. The antithesis of mind and matter is, as we have seen, more or less illusory; but there is another antithesis which is more important — that, namely, between things that can be affected by our desires and things that cannot be so affected. The line between the two is neither sharp nor immutable — as science advances, more and more things are brought under human control. Nevertheless there remain things definitely on the other side. Among these are all the *large* facts of our world, the sort of facts that are dealt with by astronomy. It is only facts on or near the surface of the earth that we can, to some extent, mould to suit our desires. And even on the surface of the earth our powers are very limited. Above all, we cannot prevent death, although we can often delay it.

Religion is an attempt to overcome this antithesis. If the world is controlled by God, and God can be moved by prayer, we acquire a share in omnipotence. In former days, miracles happened in answer to prayer; they still do in the Catholic Church, but Protestants have lost this power. However, it is possible to dispense with miracles, since Providence has decreed that the operation of natural laws shall produce the best possible results. Thus belief in God still serves to humanise the world of nature, and to make men feel that physical forces are really their allies. In like manner immortality removes the terror from death. People who believe that when they die they will inherit eternal bliss may be expected to view death without horror, though, fortunately for medical men, this does not invariably happen. It does, however, soothe men's fears somewhat even when it cannot allay them wholly.

Religion, since it has its source in terror, has dignified certain kinds of fear, and made people think them not disgraceful. In this it has done mankind a great disservice: *all* fear is bad. I believe that when I die I shall rot, and nothing of my ego will survive. I am not young, and I love life. But I should scorn to shiver with terror at the thought of annihilation. Happiness is none the less true happiness because it must come to an end, nor do thought and love lose their value because they are not everlasting. Many a man has borne himself proudly on the scaffold; surely the same pride should teach us to think truly about man's place in the world. Even if the open windows of science at first make us shiver after the cosy indoor warmth of traditional humanising myths, in the end the fresh air brings vigour, and the great spaces have a splendour of their own.

The philosophy of nature is one thing, the philosophy of value is quite another. Nothing but harm can come of confusing them. What we think good, what we should like, has no bearing whatever upon what is, which is the question for the philosophy of nature. On the other hand, we cannot be forbidden to value this or that on the ground that the nonhuman world does not value it, nor can we be compelled to admire anything because it is a 'law of nature'. Undoubtedly we are part of nature, which has produced our desires, our hopes and fears, in accordance with laws which the physicist is beginning to discover. In this sense we are part of nature, we are subordinated to nature, the outcome of natural laws, and their victims in the long run.

The philosophy of nature must not be unduly terrestrial; for it, the earth is merely one of the smaller planets of one of the smaller stars of the Milky Way. It would be ridiculous to warp the philosophy of nature in order to bring out results that are pleasing to the tiny parasites of this insignificant planet. Vitalism as a philosophy, and evolutionism, show, in this respect, a lack of sense of proportion and logical relevance. They regard the facts of life, which are personally interesting to us, as having a cosmic significance, not a significance confined to the earth's surface. Optimism and pessimism, as cosmic philosophies, show the same naïve humanism; the great world, so far as we know it from the philosophy of nature, is neither good nor bad, and is not concerned to make us happy or unhappy. All such philosophies spring from self-importance, and are best corrected by a little astronomy.

But in the philosophy of value the situation is reversed. Nature is only a part of what we can imagine; everything, real or imagined, can be appraised by us, and there is no outside standard to show that our valuation is wrong. We are ourselves the ultimate and irrefutable arbiters of value, and in the world of value Nature is only a part. Thus in this world we are greater than Nature. In the world of values, Nature in itself is neutral, neither good nor bad, deserving of neither admiration nor censure. It is we who create value and our desires which confer value. In this realm we are kings, and we debase our kingship if we bow down to Nature. It is for us to determine the good life, not for Nature — not even for Nature personified as God.

# 2

# THE GOOD LIFE

There have been at different times and among different people many varying conceptions of the good life. To some extent the differences were amenable to argument; this was when men differed as to the means to achieve a given end. Some think that prison is a good way of preventing crime; others hold that education would be better. A difference of this sort can be decided by sufficient evidence. But some differences cannot be tested in this way. Tolstoy condemned all war; others have held the life of a soldier doing battle for the right to be very noble. Here there was probably involved a real difference as to ends. Those who praise the soldier usually consider the punishment of sinners a good thing in itself; Tolstoy did not think so. On such a matter no argument is possible. I cannot, therefore, prove that my view of the good life is right; I can only state my view, and hope that as many as possible will agree. My view is this:

> The good life is one inspired by love and guided by knowledge.

Knowledge and love are both indefinitely extensible; therefore, however good a life may be, a better life can be imagined. Neither love without knowledge, nor knowledge without love can produce a good life. In the Middle Ages, when pestilence appeared in a country, holy men advised the population to assemble in churches and pray for deliverance; the result was that the infection spread with extraordinary rapidity among the crowded masses of supplicants. This was an example of love, without knowledge. The late war afforded an example of knowledge without love. In each case, the result was death on a large scale.

Although both love and knowledge are necessary, love is in a sense more fundamental, since it will lead intelligent people to seek knowledge, in order to find out how to benefit those whom they love. But if people are not intelligent, they will be content to believe what they have been told, and may do harm in spite of the most genuine benevolence. Medicine affords, perhaps, the best example of what I mean. An able physician is more useful to a patient than the most devoted friend, and progress in medical knowledge does more for the health of the community than ill-informed philanthropy. Nevertheless, an element of benevolence is essential even here if any but the rich are to profit by scientific discoveries.

Love is a word which covers a variety of feelings; I have used it purposely, as I wish to include them all. Love as an emotion — which is what I am speaking about, for love ‘on principle’ does not seem to me genuine — moves between two poles: on one side, pure delight in contemplation; on the other, pure benevolence. Where inanimate objects are concerned, delight alone enters in; we cannot feel benevolence towards a landscape or a sonata. This type of enjoyment is presumably the source of art. It is stronger, as a rule, in very young children than in adults, who are apt to view objects in a utilitarian spirit. It plays a large part in our feelings towards human beings, some of whom have charm and some the reverse, when considered simply as objects of aesthetic contemplation.

The opposite pole of love is pure benevolence. Men have sacrificed their lives to helping lepers; in such a case the love they felt cannot have had any element of aesthetic delight. Parental affection, as a rule, is accompanied by pleasure in the child’s appearance, but remains strong when this element is wholly absent. It would seem odd to call a mother’s interest in a sick child ‘benevolence’, because we are in the habit of using this word to describe a pale emotion nine parts humbug. But it is difficult to find any other word to describe the desire for another person's welfare. It is a fact that a desire of this sort may reach any degree of strength in the case of parental feeling. In other cases it is far less intense; indeed it would seem likely that all altruistic emotion is a sort of overflow of parental feeling, or sometimes a sublimation of it. For want of a better word, I shall call this emotion 'benevolence'. But I want to make it clear that I am speaking of an emotion, not a principle, and that I do not include in it any feeling of superiority such as is sometimes associated with the word. The word 'sympathy' expresses part of what I mean, but leaves out the element of activity that I wish to include.

Love at its fullest is an indissoluble combination of the two elements, delight and well-wishing. The pleasure of a parent in a beautiful and successful child combines both elements; so does sex-love at its best. But in sex-love benevolence will only exist where there is secure possession, since otherwise jealousy will destroy it, while perhaps actually increasing the delight in contemplation.

Delight without well-wishing may be cruel; well-wishing without delight easily tends to become cold and a little superior. A person who wishes to be loved wishes to be the object of a love containing both elements, except in cases of extreme weakness, such as infancy and severe illness. In these cases benevolence may be all that is desired. Conversely, in cases of extreme strength, admiration is more desired than benevolence: this is the state of mind of potentates and famous beauties. We only desire other people's good wishes in proportion as we feel ourselves in need of help or in danger of harm from them. At least, that would seem to be the biological logic of the situation, but it is not quite true to life. We desire affection in order to escape from the feeling of loneliness, in order to be, as we say, 'understood'. This is a matter of sympathy, not merely of benevolence; the person whose affection is satisfactory to us must not merely wish us well, but must know in what our happiness consists. But this belongs to the other element of the good life, namely knowledge.

In a perfect world, every sentient being would be to

every other the object of the fullest love, compounded of delight, benevolence, and understanding inextricably blended. It does not follow that, in this actual world, we ought to attempt to have such feelings towards all the sentient beings whom we encounter. There are many in whom we cannot feel delight, because they are disgusting; if we were to do violence to our nature by trying to see beauties in them, we should merely blunt our susceptibilities to what we naturally find beautiful. Not to mention human beings there are fleas and bugs and lice. We should have to be as hard pressed as the Ancient Mariner before we could feel delight in contemplating these creatures. Some saints, it is true, have called them 'pearls of God', but what these men delighted in was the opportunity of displaying their own sanctity.

Benevolence is easier to extend widely, but even benevolence has its limits. If a man wished to marry a lady, we should not think the better of him for withdrawing if he found that someone else also wished to marry her: we should regard this as a fair field for competition. Yet his feelings towards a rival cannot be *wholly* benevolent. I think that in all descriptions of the good life here on earth we must assume a certain basis of animal vitality and animal instinct; without this, life becomes tame and uninteresting. Civilisation should be something added to this, not substituted for it; the ascetic saint and the detached sage fail in this respect to be complete human beings. A small number of them may enrich a community; but a world composed of them would die of boredom.

These considerations lead to a certain emphasis on the element of delight as an ingredient in the best love. Delight, in this actual world, is unavoidably selective, and prevents us from having the same feelings towards all mankind. When conflicts arise between delight and benevolence, they must, as a rule, be decided by a compromise, not by a complete surrender of either. Instinct has its rights, and if we do violence to it beyond a point it takes vengeance in subtle ways. Therefore in aiming at a good life the limits of human possibility must be borne in mind. Here again, however, we are brought back to the necessity of knowledge.

When I speak of knowledge as an ingredient of the good life, I am not thinking of ethical knowledge, but of scientific knowledge and knowledge of particular facts. I do not think there is, strictly speaking, such a thing as ethical knowledge. If we desire to achieve some end, knowledge may show us the means, and this knowledge may loosely pass as ethical. But I do not believe that we can decide what sort of conduct is right or wrong except by reference to its probable consequences. Given an end to be achieved, it is a question for science to discover how to achieve it. All moral rules must be tested by examining whether they tend to realise ends that we desire. I say ends that we desire, not ends that we *ought* to desire. What we 'ought' to desire is merely what someone else wishes us to desire. Usually it is what the authorities wish us to desire — parents, school-masters, policemen, and judges. If you say to me 'you ought to do so-and-so', the motive power of your remark lies in my desire for your approval —

together, possibly, with rewards or punishments attached to your approval or disapproval. Since all behaviour springs from desire, it is clear that ethical notions can have no importance except as they influence desire. They do this through the desire for approval and the fear of disapproval. These are powerful social forces, and we shall naturally endeavour to win them to our side if we wish to realise any social purpose. When I say that the morality of conduct is to be judged by its probable consequences, I mean that I desire to see approval given to behaviour likely to realise social purposes which we desire, and disapproval to opposite behaviour. At present this is not done; there are certain traditional rules according to which approval and disapproval are meted out quite regardless of consequences. But this is a topic with which we shall deal in the next section.

The superfluity of theoretical ethics is obvious in simple cases. Suppose, for instance, your child is ill. Love makes you wish to cure it, and science tells you how to do so. There is not an intermediate stage of ethical theory, where it is demonstrated that your child had better be cured. Your act springs directly from desire for an end, together with knowledge of means. This is equally true of all acts, whether good or bad. The ends differ, and the knowledge is more adequate in some cases than in others. But there is no conceivable way of making people do things they do not wish to do. What is possible is to alter their desires by a system of rewards and penalties, among which social approval and disapproval are not the least potent. The question for the legislative moralist is, therefore: How shall this system of rewards and punishments be arranged so as to secure the maximum of what is desired by the legislative authority? If I say that the legislative authority has bad desires, I mean merely that its desires conflict with those of some section of the community to which I belong. Outside human desires there is no moral standard.

Thus, what distinguishes ethics from science is not any special kind of knowledge but merely desire. The knowledge required in ethics is exactly like the knowledge elsewhere; what is peculiar is that certain ends are desired, and that right conduct is what conduces to them. Of course, if the definition of right conduct is to make a wide appeal, the ends must be such as large sections of mankind desire. If I defined right conduct as that which increases my own income, readers would disagree. The whole effectiveness of any ethical argument lies in its scientific part, i. e. in the proof that one kind of conduct, rather than some other, is a means to an end which is widely desired. I distinguish, however, between ethical argument and ethical education. The latter consists in strengthening certain desires and weakening others. This is quite a different process, which will be separately discussed at a later stage.

We can now explain more exactly the purport of the definition of the good life with which this chapter began. When I said that the good life consists of love guided by knowledge, the desire which prompted me was the desire to live such a life as far as possible, and to see others living it; and the logical content of the statement is that, in a community where men live in this way, more desires will be satisfied than in one where there is less love or less knowledge. I do not mean that such a life is 'virtuous' or that its opposite is 'sinful', for these are conceptions which seem to me to have no scientific justification.

# 3

# MORAL RULES

The practical need of morals arises from the conflict of desires, whether of different people or of the same person at different times or even at one time. A man desires to drink, and also to be fit for his work next morning. We think him immoral if he adopts the course which gives him the smaller total satisfaction of desire. We think ill of people who are extravagant or reckless, even if they injure no one but themselves. Bentham supposed that the whole of morality could be derived from ‘enlightened self-interest', and that a person who always acted with a view to his own maximum satisfaction in the long run would always act rightly. I cannot accept this view. Tyrants have existed who derived exquisite pleasure from watching the infliction of torture; I cannot praise such men when prudence led them to spare their victims' lives with a view to further sufferings another day. Nevertheless, other things being equal, prudence is a part of the good life. Even Robinson Crusoe had occasion to practise industry, self-control and foresight which must be reckoned as moral qualities, since they increased his total satisfaction without counterbalancing injury to others. This part of morals plays a great part in the training of young children, who have little inclination to think of the future. If it were more practised in later life, the world would quickly become a paradise, since it would be quite sufficient to prevent wars, which are acts of passion, not reason. Nevertheless, in spite of the importance of prudence, it is not the most interesting part of morals. Nor is it the part that raises intellectual problems, since it does not require an appeal to anything beyond self-interest.

The part of morality that is not included in prudence, is, in essence, analogous to law, or the rules of a club. It is a method of enabling men to live together in a community in spite of the possibility that their desires may conflict. But here two very different methods are possible. There is the method of criminal law, which aims at a merely external harmony by attaching disagreeable consequences to acts which thwart other men's desires in certain ways. This is also the method of social censure: to be thought ill of by one's own society is a form of punishment, to avoid which most people avoid being known to transgress the code of their set. But there is another method, more fundamental, and far more satisfactory when it succeeds. This is to alter men's characters and desires in such a way as to minimise occasions of conflict by making the success of one man's desires as far as possible consistent with that of another's. That is why love is better than hate, because it brings harmony instead of conflict into the desires of the person concerned. Two people between whom there is love succeed or fail together, but when two people hate each other the success of either is the failure of the other.

If we were right in saying that the good life is inspired by love and guided by knowledge, it is clear that the moral code of any community is not ultimate and self-sufficient, but must be examined with a view to seeing whether it is such as wisdom and benevolence would have decreed. Moral codes have not always been faultless. The Aztecs considered it their painful duty to eat human flesh for fear the light of the sun should grow dim. They erred in their science; and perhaps they would have perceived the scientific error if they had had any love for the sacrificial victims. Some tribes immure girls in the dark from the age of 10 to the age of 17, for fear the sun's rays should render them pregnant. But surely our modern codes of morals contain nothing analogous to these savage practices? Surely we only forbid things which are really harmful, or at any rate so abominable that no decent person could defend them? I am not so sure.

Current morality is a curious blend of utilitarianism

and superstition, but the superstitious part has the stronger hold, as is natural, since superstition is the origin of moral rules. Originally, certain acts were thought displeasing to the gods, and were forbidden by law because the divine wrath was apt to descend upon the community, not merely upon the guilty individuals. Hence arose the conception of sin, as that which is displeasing to God. No reason can be assigned as to why certain acts should be thus displeasing; it would be very difficult to say, for instance, why it was displeasing that the kid should be seethed in its mother's milk. But it was known by Revelation that this was the case. Sometimes the Divine commands have been curiously interpreted. For example, we are told not to work on Saturdays, and Protestants take this to mean that we are not to play on Sundays. But the same sublime authority is attributed to the new prohibition as to the old.

It is evident that a man with a scientific outlook on life cannot let himself be intimidated by texts of Scripture or by the teaching of the Church. He will not be content to say 'such-and-such an act is sinful, and that ends the matter'.

He will inquire whether it does any harm or whether, on the contrary, the belief that it is sinful does harm. And he will find that, especially in what concerns sex, our current morality contains a very great deal of which the origin is purely superstitious. He will find also that this superstition, like that of the Aztecs, involves needless cruelty, and would be swept away if people were actuated by kindly feelings towards their neighbours. But the defenders of traditional morality are seldom people with warm hearts, as may be seen from the love of militarism displayed by Church dignitaries. One is tempted to think that they value morals as affording a legitimate outlet for their desire to inflict pain; the sinner is fair game, and therefore away with tolerance!

Let us follow an ordinary human life from conception to the grave, and note the points where superstitious morals inflict preventable suffering. I begin with conception, because here the influence of superstition is particularly noteworthy. If the parents are not married, the child has a stigma, as clearly undeserved as anything could be. If either of the parents has venereal disease, the child is likely to inherit it. If they already have too many children for the family income, there will be poverty, underfeeding, overcrowding, very likely incest. Yet the great majority of moralists agree that the parents had better not know how to preven this misery by preventing conception.'[1] To please these moralists, a life of torture is inflicted upon millions of human beings who ought never to have existed, merely because it is supposed that sexual intercourse is wicked unless accompanied by desire for offspring, but not wicked when this desire is present, even though the offspring is humanly certain to be wretched. To be killed suddenly and then eaten, which was the fate of the Aztecs' victims, is a far less degree of suffering than is inflicted upon a child born in miserable surroundings and

---

① This is fortunately no longer true. The vast majority of Protestant and Jewish leaders do not now object to birth control. Russell's statement is a perfectly accurate description of conditions in 1925. It is also significant that, with one or two excep-tions, all the great pioneers of contraception — Francis Place, Richard Carlile, Charles Knowlton, Charles Bradlaugh and Margaret Sanger — were prominent Free-thinkers. (Editor's note.)

tainted with venereal disease. Yet it is the greater suffering which is deliberately inflicted by bishops and politicians in the name of morality. If they had even the smallest spark of love or pity for children they could not adhere to a moral code involving this fiendish cruelty.

At birth, and in early infancy, the average child suffers more from economic causes than from superstition. When well-to-do women have children, they have the best doctors, the best nurses, the best diet, the best rest and the best exercise. Working-class women do not enjoy these advantages, and frequently their children die for lack of them. A little is done by the public authorities in the way of care of mothers, but very grudgingly. At a moment when the supply of milk to nursing mothers is being cut down to save expense, public authorities will spend vast sums on paving rich residential districts where there is little traffic. They must know that in taking this decision they are condemning a certain number of working-class children to death for the crime of poverty. Yet the ruling party are supported by the immense majority of ministers of religion, who, with the Pope at their head, have pledged the vast forces of superstition throughout the world to the support of social injustice.

In all stages of education the influence of superstition is disastrous. A certain percentage of children have the habit of thinking; one of the aims of education is to cure them of this habit. Inconvenient questions are met with 'hush, hush', or with punishment. Collective emotion is used to instil certain kinds of belief, more particularly nationalistic kinds. Capitalists, militarists, and ecclesiastics co-operate in education, because all depend for their power upon the prevalence of emotionalism and the rarity of critical judgement. With the aid of human nature, education succeeds in increasing and intensifying these propensities of the average man.

Another way in which superstition damages education is through its influence on the choice of teachers. For economic reasons, a woman teacher must not be married; for moral reasons, she must not have extra-marital sexual relations. And yet everybody who has taken the trouble to study morbid psychology knows that prolonged virginity is, as a rule, extraordinarily harmful to women, so harmful that, in a sane society, it would be severely discouraged in teachers. The restrictions imposed lead more and more to a refusal, on the part of energetic and enterprising women, to enter the teaching profession. This is all due to the lingering influence of superstitious asceticism.

At middle and upper class schools the matter is even worse. There are chapel services, and the care of morals is in the hands of clergymen. Clergymen, almost necessarily, fail in two ways as teachers of morals. They condemn acts which do not harm and they condone acts which do great harm. They all condemn sexual relations between unmarried people who are fond of each other but not yet sure that they wish to live together all their lives. Most of them condemn birth control. None of them condemns the brutality of a husband who causes his wife to die of too frequent pregnancies. I knew a fashionable clergyman whose wife had nine children in nine years. The doctors told him that if she had another she would die. Next year she had another and died. No one condemned; he retained his benefice and married again. So long as clergymen continue to condone cruelty and condemn innocent pleasure, they can only do harm as guardians of the morals of the young.

Another bad effect of superstition on education is the absence of instruction about the facts of sex. The main physiological facts ought to be taught quite simply and naturally before puberty at a time when they are not exciting. At puberty, the elements of an unsupers-titious sexual morality ought to be taught. Boys and girls should be taught that nothing can justify sexual intercourse unless there is mutual inclination. This is contrary to the teaching of the Church, which holds that, provided the parties are married and the man desires another child, sexual intercourse is justified however great may be the reluctance of the wife. Boys and girls should be taught respect for each other's liberty; they should be made to feel that nothing gives one human being rights over another, and that jealousy and possessiveness kill love. They should be taught that to bring another human being into the world is a very serious matter, only to be undertaken when the child will have a reasonable prospect of health, good surroundings, and parental care. But they should also be taught methods of birth control, so as to insure that children shall only come when they are wanted. Finally, they should be taught the dangers of venereal disease, and the methods of prevention and cure. The increase of human happiness to be expected from sex education on these lines is immeasurable.

It should be recognised that, in the absence of children, sexual relations are a purely private matter, which does not concern either the State or the neighbours. Certain forms of sex which do not lead to children are at present punished by the criminal law: this is purely superstitious, since the matter is one which affects no one except the parties directly concerned. Where there are children, it is a mistake to suppose that it is necessarily to their interest to make divorce very difficult. Habitual drunkenness, cruelty, insanity are grounds upon which divorce is necessary for the children's sake quite as much as for the sake of the wife or husband. The peculiar importance attached, at present, to adultery is quite irrational. It is obvious that many forms of misconduct are more fatal to married happiness than an occasional infidelity. Masculine insistence on a child a year, which is not conventionally misconduct or cruelty, is the most fatal of all.

Moral rules ought not to be such as to make instinctive happiness impossible. Yet that is an effect of strict monogamy in a community where the numbers of the two sexes are very unequal. Of course, under such circumstances, the moral rules are infringed. But when the rules are such that they can only be obeyed by greatly diminishing the happiness of the community, and when it is better they should be infringed than observed, surely it is time that the rules were changed. If this is not done, many people who are acting in a way not contrary to the public interest are faced with the undeserved alternative of hypocrisy or obloquy. The Church does not mind hypocrisy, which is a flattering tribute to its power; but elsewhere it has come to be recognised as an evil which we ought not lightly to inflict.

Even more harmful than theological superstition is the superstition of nationalism, of duty to one's own State and to no other. But I do not propose on this occasion to discuss the matter beyond pointing out that limitation to one's compatriots is contrary to the principle of love which we recognised as constituting the good life. It is also, of course, contrary to enlightened self-interest, since an exclusive nationalism does not pay even the victorious nations.

One other respect in which our society suffers from the theological conception of 'sin' is the treatment of criminals. The view that criminals are 'wicked' and 'deserve' punishment is not one which a rational morality can support. Undoubtedly certain people do things which society wishes to prevent, and does right in preventing as far as possible. We may take murder as the plainest case. Obviously, if a community is to hold together and we are to enjoy its pleasures and advantages, we cannot allow people to kill each other whenever they feel an impulse to do so. But this problem should be treated in a purely scientific spirit. We should ask simply: What is the best method of preventing murder? Of two methods which are equally effective in preventing murder, the one involving least harm to the murderer is to be preferred. The harm to the murderer is wholly regrettable, like the pain of a surgical operation. It may be equally necessary, but it is not a subject for rejoicing. The vindictive feeling called 'moral indignation' is merely a form of cruelty. Suffering to the criminal can never be justified by the notion of vindictive punishment. If education combined with kindness is equally effective, it is to be preferred; still more is it to be preferred if it is more effective. Of course, the prevention of crime and the punishment of crime are two different questions; the object of causing pain to the criminal is presumably deterrent. If prisons were so humanised that a prisoner got a good education for nothing, people might commit crimes in order to qualify for entrance. No doubt prison must be less pleasant than freedom; but the best way to secure this result is to make freedom more pleasant than it sometimes is at present. I do not wish, however, to embark upon the subject of Penal Reform. I merely wish to suggest that we should treat the criminal as we treat a man suffering from plague. Each is a public danger, each must have his liberty curtailed until he has ceased to be a danger. But the man suffering from plague is an object of sympathy and commiseration, whereas the criminal is an object of execration. This is quite irrational. And it is because of this difference of attitude that our prisons are so much less successful in curing criminal tendencies than our hospitals are in curing disease.

# 4

# SALVATION

## Individual and social

One of the defects of traditional religion is its individualism, and this defect belongs also to the morality associated with it. Traditionally, the religious life was, as it were, a duologue between the soul and God. To obey the will of God was virtue; and this was possible for the individual quite regardless of the state of the community. Protestant sects developed the idea of 'finding salvation', but it was always present in Christian teaching. This individualism of the separate soul had its value at certain stages of history, but in the modern world we need rather a social than an individual conception of welfare. I want to consider, in this section, how this affects our conception of the good life.

Christianity arose in the Roman Empire among populations, wholly destitute of political power, whose national States had been destroyed and merged in a vast impersonal aggregate. During the first three centuries of the Christian era the individuals who adopted Christianity could not alter the social or political institutions under which they lived, although they were profoundly convinced of their badness. In these circumstances, it was natural that they should adopt the belief that an individual may be perfect in an imperfect world, and that the good life has nothing to do with this world. What I mean may become plain by comparison with Plato's Republic. When Plato wanted to describe the good life, he described a whole community, not an individual; he did so in order to define justice, which is an essentially social conception. He was accustomed to citizenship of a republic, and political responsibility was something which he took for granted. With the loss of Greek freedom comes the rise of Stoicism, which is like Christianity, and unlike Plato, in having an individualistic conception of the good life.

We, who belong to great democracies, should find a more appropriate morality in free Athens than in despotic Imperial Rome. In India, where the political circumstances are very similar to those of Judea in the time of Christ, we find Gandhi preaching a very similar morality to Christ's and being punished for it by the christianised successors of Pontius Pilate. But the more extreme Indian nationalists are not content with individual salvation: they want national salvation. In this they have taken on the outlook of the free democracies of the West. I want to suggest some respects in which this outlook, owing to Christian influences, is not yet sufficiently bold and selfconscious, but is still hampered by the belief in individual salvation.

The good life, as we conceive it, demands a multitude

of social conditions, and cannot be realised without them. The good life, we said, is a life inspired by love and guided by knowledge. The knowledge required can only exist where governments or millionaires devote themselves to its discovery and diffusion. For example, the spread of cancer is alarming — what are we to do about it? At the moment, no one can answer the question for lack of knowledge; and the knowledge is not likely to emerge except through endowed research. Again, knowledge of science, history, literature and art ought to be attainable by all who desire it; this requires elaborate arrangements on the part of public authorities, and is not to be achieved by means of religious conversion. Then there is foreign trade, without which half the inhabitants of Great Britain would starve; and if we were starving very few of us would live the good life. It is needless to multiply examples. The important point is that, in all that differentiates between a good life and a bad one, the world is a unity, and the man who pretends to live independently is a conscious or unconscious parasite.

The idea of individual salvation, with which the early Christians consoled themselves for their political subjection, becomes impossible as soon as we escape from a very narrow conception of the good life. In the orthodox Christian conception, the good life is the virtuous life, and virtue consists in obedience to the will of God, and the will of God is revealed to each individual through the voice of conscience. This whole conception is that of men subject to an alien despotism. The good life involves much beside virtue — intelligence, for instance. And conscience is a most fallacious guide, since it consists of vague reminiscences of precepts heard in early youth, so that it is never wiser than its possessor's nurse or mother. To live a good life in the fullest sense a man must have a good education, friends, love, children (if he desires them), a sufficient income to keep him from want and grave anxiety, good health, and work which is not uninteresting. All these things, in varying degrees, depend upon the community, and are helped or hindered by political events. The good life must be lived in a good society, and is not fully possible otherwise.

This is the fundamental defect of the aristocratic ideal. Certain good things, such as art and science and friendship, can flourish very well in an aristocratic society. They existed in Greece on a basis of slavery; they exist among ourselves on a basis of exploitation. But love, in the form of sympathy, or benevolence, cannot exist freely in an aristocratic society. The aristocrat has to persuade himself that the slave or proletarian or coloured man is of inferior clay, and that his sufferings do not matter. At the present moment, polished English gentlemen flog Africans so severely that they die after hours of unspeakable anguish. Even if these gentlemen are welleducated, artistic, and admirable conversationalists, I cannot admit that they are living the good life. Human nature imposes some limitation of sympathy, but not such a degree as that. In a democratically-minded society, only a maniac would behave in this way. The limitation of sympathy involved in the aristocratic ideal is its condemnation. Salvation is an aristocratic ideal, because it is individualistic. For this reason, also, the idea of personal salvation, however interpreted and expanded, cannot serve for the definition of the good life.

Another characteristic of salvation is that it results from a catastrophic change, like the conversion of St Paul. Shelley's poems afford an illustration of this conception applied to societies; the moment comes when everybody is converted, the 'anarchs' fly, and 'the world's great age begins anew'. It may be said that a poet is an unimportant person, whose ideas are of no consequence. But I am persuaded that a large proportion of revolutionary leaders have had ideas extremely like Shelley's. They have thought that misery and cruelty and degradation were due to tyrants or priests or capitalists or Germans, and that if these sources of evil were overthrown there would be a general change of heart and we should all live happy ever after. Holding these beliefs, they have been willing to wage a 'war to end war'. Comparatively fortunate were those who had suffered defeat or death; those who had the misfortune to emerge victorious were reduced to cynicism and despair by the failure of all their glowing hopes. The ultimate source of these hopes was the Christian doctrine of catastrophic conversion as the road to salvation.

I do not wish to suggest that revolutions are never necessary, but I do wish to suggest that they are not short cuts to the millennium. There is no short cut to the good life, whether individual or social. To build up the good life, we must build up intelligence, self-control and sympathy. This is a quantitative matter, a matter of gradual improvement, of early training, of educational experiment. Only impatience prompts the belief in the possibility of sudden improvement. The gradual improvement that is possible, and the methods by which it may be achieved, are a matter for future science. But something can be said now. Some part of what can be said I shall try to indicate in a final section.

# 5

# SCIENCE AND HAPPINESS

The purpose of the moralist is to improve men's behaviour. This is a laudable ambition, since their behaviour is for the most part deplorable. But I cannot praise the moralist either for the particular improvements he desires or for the methods he adopts for achieving them. His ostensible method is moral exhortation; his real method (if he is orthodox) is a system of economic rewards and punishments. The former effects nothing permanent or important; the influence of revivalists, from Savonarola downwards, has always been very transitory. The latter — the rewards and punishments — have a very considerable effect. They cause a man, for example, to prefer casual prostitutes to a quasi-permanent mistress, because it is necessary to adopt the method which is most easily concealed. They thus keep up the numbers of a very dangerous profession, and secure the prevalence of venereal disease. These are not the objects desired by the moralist, and he is too unscientific to notice that they are the objects which he actually achieves.

Is there anything better to be substituted for this unscientific mixture of preaching and bribery? I think there is.

Men's actions are harmful either from ignorance or from bad desires. 'Bad' desires, when we are speaking from a social point of view, may be defined as those which tend to thwart the desires of others, or more exactly, those which thwart more desires than they assist. It is not necessary to dwell upon the harmfulness that springs from ignorance; here, more knowledge is all that is wanted, so that the road to improvement lies in more research and more education. But the harmfulness that springs from bad desires is a more difficult matter.

In the ordinary man and woman there is a certain amount of active malevolence, both special ill-will directed to particular enemies and general impersonal pleasure in the misfortunes of others. It is customary to cover this over with fine phrases; about half of conventional morality is a cloak for it. But it must be faced if the moralists' aim of improving our actions is to be achieved. It is shown in a thousand ways, great and small: in the glee with which people repeat and believe scandal, in the unkind treatment of criminals in spite of clear proof that better treatment would have more effect in reforming them, in the unbelievable barbarity with which all white races treat Negroes, and in the gusto with which old ladies and clergymen pointed out the duty of military service to young men during the War. Even children may be the objects of wanton cruelty: David Copperfield and Oliver Twist are by no means imaginary. This active malevolence is the worst feature of human nature and the one which it is most necessary to change if the world is to grow happier. Probably this one cause has more to do with war than all the economic and political causes put together.

Given this problem of preventing malevolence, how shall we deal with it? First let us try to understand its causes. These are, I think, pardy social, partly physiological. The world, now as much as at any former time, is based upon life-and-death competition; the question at issue in the War was whether German or Allied children should die of want and starvation. (Apart from malevolence on both sides there was not the slightest reason why both should not survive.) Most people have in the background of their minds a haunting fear of ruin; this is especially true of people who have children. The rich fear that Bolsheviks will confiscate their investments; the poor fear that they will lose their job or their health. Everyone is engaged in the frantic pursuit of 'security' and imagines that this is to be achieved by keeping potential enemies in subjection. It is in moments of panic that cruelty becomes most widespread and most atrocious. Reactionaries everywhere appeal to fear: in England, to fear of Bolshevism; in France, to fear of Germany; in Germany, to fear of France. And the sole effect of their appeals is to increase the danger against which they wish to be protected.

It must, therefore, be one of the chief concerns of the scientific moralist to combat fear. This can be done in two ways: by increasing security, and by cultivating courage. I am speaking of fear as an irrational passion, not of the rational prevision of possible misfortune. When a theatre catches fire, the rational man foresees disaster just as clearly as the man stricken with panic, but he adopts methods likely to diminish the disaster, whereas the man stricken with panic increases it. Europe since 1914 has been like a panic-stricken audience in a theatre on fire; what is needed is calm, authoritative directions as to how to escape without trampling each other to pieces in the process. The Victorian Age, for all its humbug, was a period of rapid progress, because men were dominated by hope rather than fear. If we are again to have progress, we must again be dominated by hope.

Everything that increases the general security is likely to diminish cruelty. This applies to prevention of war, whether through the instrumentality of the League of Nations or otherwise; to prevention of destitution; to better health by improvement in medicine, hygiene, and sanitation; and to all other methods of lessening the terrors that lurk in the abysses of men's minds and emerge as nightmares when they sleep. But nothing is accomplished by an attempt to make a portion of mankind secure at the expense of another portion — Frenchmen at the expense of Germans, capitalists at the expense of wage-earners, white men at the expense of yellow men, and so on. Such methods only increase terror in the dominant group, lest just resentment should lead the oppressed to rebel. Only justice can give security; and by 'justice' I mean the recognition of the equal claims of all human beings.

In addition to social changes designed to bring security there is, however, another and more direct means of diminishing fear, namely by a regimen designed to increase courage. Owing to the importance of courage in battle, men early discovered means of increasing it by education and diet — eating human flesh, for example, was supposed to be useful. But military courage was to be the prerogative of the ruling caste: Spartans were to have more than helots, British officers than Indian privates, men than women, and so on. For centuries it was supposed to be the privilege of the aristocracy. Every increase of courage in the ruling caste was used to increase the burdens on the oppressed, and therefore to increase the grounds for fear in the oppressors, and therefore to leave the causes of cruelty undiminished. Courage must be democratised before it can make men humane.

To a great extent, courage has already been democratised by recent events. The suffragettes showed that they possessed as much courage as the bravest men; this demonstration was essential in winning them the vote. The common soldier in the War needed as much courage as a captain or lieutenant, and much more than a general; this had much to do with his lack of servility after demobilisation. The Bolsheviks, who proclaim themselves the champions of the proletariat, are not lacking in courage, whatever else may be said of them; this is proved by their pre-revolutionary record. In Japan, where formerly the Samurai had a monopoly of martial ardour, conscription brought the need of courage throughout the male population. Thus among all the Great Powers much has been done during the past half-century to make courage no longer an aristocratic monopoly: if this were not the case, the danger to democracy would be far greater than it is.

But courage in fighting is by no means the only form, nor perhaps even the most important. There is courage in facing poverty, courage in facing derision, courage in facing the hostility of one's own herd. In these, the bravest soldiers are often lamentably deficient. And above all there is the courage to think calmly and rationally in the face of danger, and to control the impulse of panic fear or panic rage. These are certainly things which education can help to give. And the teaching of every form of courage is rendered easier by good health, good physique, adequate nourishment, and free play for fundamental vital impulses. Perhaps the physiological sources of courage could be discovered by comparing the blood of a cat with that of a rabbit. In all likelihood there is no limit to what science could do in the way of increasing courage, by example, experience of danger, an athletic life, and a suitable diet. All these things our upper class boys to a great extent enjoy, but as yet they are in the main the prerogative of wealth. The courage so far encouraged in the poorer sections of the community is courage under orders, not the kind that involves initiative and leadership. When the qualities that now confer leadership have become universal, there will no longer be leaders and followers, and democracy will have been realised at last.

But fear is not the only source of malevolence; envy and disappointment also have their share. The envy of cripples and hunchbacks is proverbial as a source of malignity, but other misfortunes than theirs produce similar results. A man or woman who has been thwarted sexually is apt to be full of envy; this generally takes the form of moral condemnation of the more fortunate. Much of the driving force of revolutionary movements is due to envy of the rich. Jealousy is, of course, a special form of envy — envy of love. The old often envy the young; when they do, they are apt to treat them cruelly.

There is, so far as I know, no way of dealing with envy except to make the lives of the envious happier and fuller, and to encourage in youth the idea of collective enterprises rather than competition. The worst forms of envy are in those who have not had a full life in the way of marriage, or children, or career. Such misfortunes could in most cases be avoided by better social institutions. Still, it must be admitted that a residuum of envy is likely to remain. There are many instances in history of generals so jealous of each other that they preferred defeat to enhancement of the other's reputation. Two politicians of the same party, or two artists of the same school, are almost sure to be jealous of one another. In such cases, there seems nothing to be done except to arrange, as far as possible, that each competitor shall be unable to injure the other, and shall only be able to win by superior merit. An artist's jealousy of a rival does little harm usually, because the only effective way of indulging it is to paint better pictures than his rival's, since it is not open to him to destroy his rival's pictures. Where envy is unavoidable it must be used as a stimulus to one's own efforts, not to the thwarting of the efforts of rivals.

The possibilities of science in the way of increasing human happiness are not confined to diminishing those aspects of human nature which make for mutual defeat, and which we therefore call 'bad'. There is probably no limit to what science can do in the way of increasing positive excellence. Health has already been greatly improved; in spite of the lamentations of those who idealise the past, we live longer and have fewer illnesses than any class or nation in the eighteenth century. With a little more application of the knowledge we already possess, we might be much healthier than we are. And future discoveries are likely to accelerate this process enormously.

So far, it has been physical science that has had most effect upon our lives, but in the future physiology and psychology are likely to be far more potent. When we have discovered how character depends upon physiological conditions, we shall be able, if we choose, to produce far more of the type of human being that we admire. Intelligence, artistic capacity, benevolence — all these things no doubt could be increased by science. There seems scarcely any limit to what *could* be done in the way of producing a good world, if only men would use science wisely. I have expressed elsewhere my fears that men may not make a wise use of the power they derive from science.[①] At present I am concerned with the good that men could do if they chose, not with the question whether they will choose rather to do harm.

There is a certain attitude about the application of science to human life with which I have some sympathy,

---

① See *Icarus*.

though I do not, in the last analysis, agree with it. It is the attitude of those who dread what is 'unnatural'. Rousseau is, of course, the great protagonist of this view in Europe. In Asia, Lao-Tze has set it forth even more persuasively, and 2400 years sooner. I think there is a mixture of truth and falsehood in the admiration of 'nature', which it is important to disentangle. To begin with, what is 'natural'? Roughly speaking, anything to which the speaker was accustomed in childhood. Lao-Tze objects to roads and carriages and boats, all of which were probably unknown in the village where he was born. Rousseau has got used to these things, and does not regard them as against nature. But he would no doubt have thundered against railways if he had lived to see them. Clothes and cooking are too ancient to be denounced by most of the apostles of nature, though they all object to new fashions in either. Birth control is thought wicked by people who tolerate celibacy, because the former is a new violation of nature and the latter an ancient one. In all these ways those who preach nature' are inconsistent, and one is tempted to regard them as mere conservatives.

Nevertheless, there is something to be said in their favour. Take for instance vitamins, the discovery of which has produced a revulsion in favour of 'natural' foods. It seems, however, that vitamins can be supplied by cod liver oil and electric light, which are certainly not part of the 'natural' diet of a human being. This case illustrates that, in the absence of knowledge, unexpected harm may be done by a new departure from nature; but when the harm has come to be understood it can usually be remedied by some new artificiality. As regards our physical environment and our physical means of gratifying our desires, I do not think the doctrine of 'nature' justifies anything beyond a certain experimental caution in the adoption of new expedients. Clothes, for instance, are contrary to nature, and need to be supple-mented by another unnatural practice, namely washing, if they are not to bring disease. But the two practices toge-ther make a man healthier than the savage who eschews both.

There is more to be said for 'nature' in the realm of

human desires. To force upon man, woman or child a life which thwarts their strongest impulses is both cruel and dangerous; in this sense, a life according to 'nature' is to be commended with certain provisos. Nothing could be more artificial than an underground electric railway, but no violence is done to a child's nature when it is taken to travel in one; on the contrary, almost all children find the experience delightful. Artificialities which gratify the desires of ordinary human beings are good, other things being equal. But there is nothing to be said for ways of life which are artificial in the sense of being imposed by authority or economic necessity. Such ways of life are, no doubt, to some extent necessary at present; ocean travel would become very difficult if there were no stokers on steamers. But necessities of this kind are regrettable, and we ought to look for ways of avoiding them. A certain amount of work is not a thing to complain of; indeed, in nine cases out of ten, it makes a man happier than complete idleness. But the amount and kind of work that most people have to do at present is a grave evil: especially bad is the life-long bondage to routine. Life should not be too closely regulated or too methodical; our impulses, when not positively destructive or injurious to others, ought if possible to have free play; there should be room for adventure. Human nature we should respect, because our impulses and desires are the stuff out of which our happiness is to be made. It is no use to give men something abstractedly considered 'good'; we must give them something desired or needed if we are to add to their happiness. Science may learn in time to mould our desires so that they shall not conflict with those of other people to the same extent as they do now; then we shall be able to satisfy a larger proportion of our desires than at present. In that sense, but in that sense only, our desires will then have become 'better'. A single desire is no better and no worse, considered in isolation, than any other; but a group of desires is better than another group if all of the first group can be satisfied simultaneously, while in the second group some are inconsistent with others. That is why love is better than hatred.

To respect physical nature is foolish; physical nature should be studied with a view to making it serve human ends as far as possible, but it remains ethically neither good nor bad. And where physical nature and human nature interact, as in the population question, there is no need to fold our hands in passive adoration and accept war, pestilence and famine as the only possible means of dealing with excessive fertility. The divines say: it is wicked, in this matter, to apply science to the physical side of the problem; we must (they say) apply morals to the human side and practise abstinence. Apart from the fact that everyone, including the divines, knows that their advice will not be taken, why should it be wicked to solve the population question by adopting physical means for preventing conception? No answer is forthcoming except one based upon antiquated dogmas. And clearly the violence to nature advocated by the divines is at least as great as that involved in birth control. The divines prefer a violence to human nature, which, when successfully practised, involves unhappiness, envy, a tendency to persecution, often madness. I prefer a 'violence' to physical nature which is of the same sort as that involved in the steam engine or even in the use of an umbrella. This instance shows how ambiguous and uncer-tain is the application of the principle that we should follow 'nature'.

Nature, even human nature, will cease more and more to be an absolute datum; more and more it will become what scientific manipulation has made it. Science can, if it chooses, enable our grandchildren to live the good life, by giving them knowledge, self-control, and characters productive of harmony rather than strife. At present it is teaching our children to kill each other, because many men of science are willing to sacrifice the future of mankind to their own momentary prosperity. But this phase will pass when men have acquired the same domination over their own passions that they already have over the physical forces of the external world. Then at last we shall have won our freedom.

**图书在版编目(CIP)数据**

我的信念/(英)伯特兰·罗素(Bertrand Russell)著;
莫晓敏译.—上海:上海译文出版社,2018.8(2023.4重印)
(罗素文集)
书名原文:What I believe
ISBN 978-7-5327-7885-0

Ⅰ.①我… Ⅱ.①伯…②莫… Ⅲ.①罗素(Russell, Bertrand 1872-1970)—哲学思想
Ⅳ.①B561.54

中国版本图书馆CIP数据核字(2018)第136870号



图字:09-2014-963

**我的信念**
[英]伯特兰·罗素 著 莫晓敏 译
责任编辑/钟 瑾 装帧设计/半和创意

上海译文出版社有限公司出版、发行
网址:www.yiwen.com.cn
201101 上海市闵行区号景路159弄B座
杭州宏雅印刷有限公司印刷

开本 787×1092 1/32 印张 4.75 插页 5 字数 102,000
2018年8月第1版 2023年4月第4次印刷
印数:9,001—11,000册

ISBN 978-7-5327-7885-0/B·453
定价:32.00元